The
Whole Grain
Bake Book

The
Whole Grain
Bake Book

by Gail L. Worstman

Pacific Search Press

Pacific Search Press, 222 Dexter Avenue North,
    Seattle, Washington 98109
©1980 by Gail L. Worstman. All rights reserved
Printed in the United States of America

Second printing 1980
Third printing 1982

First edition published 1976 as *You Knead It:*
    A Guide to Easy Breadmaking
Second printing 1976
Third printing 1978

Edited by Miriam Remak Bulmer
Cover illustration by Liz Gong
Illustrations on pages 107–9 by Judy Petry

Library of Congress Cataloging in Publication Data
Worstman, Gail L
    The whole grain bake book.
    First ed. published in 1976 under title: You knead it.
    Includes index.
    1. Baking. 2. Cereals as food. I. Title.
TX763.W67 1979   641.6'3'1   79-14565
ISBN 0-914718-46-0

Dedicated to Keith, for the best recipe of all.

There's a little love in every loaf of bread.

Contents

Preface

Evolving from my connection with the old Wheatex Mill and its old-fashioned grain products, this book became both a labor of love and a necessity: a labor of love because I enjoy healthful foods and like to share ideas and recipes with other people; a necessity because in order to share the recipes, I had to mend my "pinch of this, dash of that, splash of something else" method of cooking and actually write down what I had kept in my head for so long. I have chosen recipes that I invented myself, favorites of my customers and friends, recipes handed down in my family, and recipes handed down within the mill itself.

I hope you will find as much pleasure in using and reading this book as I have had in writing it. Thanks go mostly to my faithful customers, without whose gentle nagging and continued interest I may never have gone beyond simply receiving their compliments about my recipes. Special thanks, also, to my family, without whose continued support and occasional rescue from impending doom this adventure would not have progressed. Thank you. I love you all. Happy baking and healthy eating!

A Guide to Easy Breadmaking

I have made bread in some fairly uncommon and strange places, such as TV studios, chemistry rooms, on the camping trail, and once, all over the back seat of my car. But since most people confine their kneading adventures to the kitchen, let's begin there.

The chances are that you already own the implements necessary for the creation of bread and you need not sink a fortune into expensive tools and gadgets. If you have the following items, you are well on the way to being fully equipped for the task: a large, nonmetallic mixing bowl; a large wooden spoon; measuring cups and spoons; a counter surface, table top, or bread board; a tea towel; a rolling pin; loaf pans, cookie sheets, and pie tins; apron; oven.

With the proper equipment, plus an understanding of the ingredients and techniques, breadmaking can be at your fingertips!

Whole Grains and Other Natural Ingredients

Breadmaking with whole grains and natural ingredients can be intimidating for the new breadmaker or for those of us who grew up in the heyday of overrefined Brand X products. The nutritional value and superior taste of whole grain products make them well worth learning about.

The Stone Buhr Method

Grains that are milled slowly, at a low temperature, on a stone mill, are said to be stone buhr ground, or simply stone-ground. This method produces finer textured flour and preserves the maximum amount of vitamins and nutrients. Most grains can be stone-ground, but very oily seeds and grains, such as soybeans or sunflower seeds, are normally hammer milled. Use stone-ground flours whenever possible, and purchase them from someone who will guarantee their freshness.

Whole Wheat Flour

Whole grain, stone-ground, hard red wheat makes the best bread flour and will produce a superb loaf. When the protein in the wheat is thirteen percent to fifteen percent, the gluten content (which makes the dough sticky and elastic) is high enough for great bread. Lower protein levels give a less elastic dough, producing a crumbly or heavy loaf. Whole wheat flour has a shelf life of two to three months, if kept in a cool, dry place, or up to six months if stored in an airtight container in the freezer.

Whole Wheat Pastry Flour

Whole grain, stone-ground, soft white wheat makes the best flour for quick breads, hot cakes, cookies, piecrusts, and other goodies. You may use it in place of unbleached flour in almost any recipe, but since it's low in gluten, don't use it for bread or kneaded pastries. A good rule to remember is, if you use baking powder, then use pastry flour; if you use yeast, use whole wheat flour.

Graham Flour

This coarse-ground, steel-cut flour contains the whole grain of wheat. Higher in bran than whole wheat flour, it is especially ideal for high roughage diets. It gives a heartier texture to bread, but you may have to knead a few minutes longer than usual to develop the gluten more fully.

Eighty-Percent Gluten Flour

That great addition to rye bread that never used to rise well, gluten flour is eighty percent gluten and is a great way to get nongluten flours to make bread that rises well. Try adding it to rye flour, rye meal, soy flour, cornmeal, potato flour, millet flour, rice flour, and others. General directions for its use are: ¼ cup of gluten flour for every 2 cups of nongluten flour in the recipe. Don't use any more than that or your bread will be good for only hockey pucks and duck decoys. To keep the gluten flour from lumping, mix it in with the flour before combining them with the other ingredients. You may also add a bit of gluten flour to unbleached flour if your bread is turning out crumbly. Add one tablespoon per cup of unbleached flour (or poor quality whole wheat flour, for that matter) to improve the texture and elasticity.

Rye, Buckwheat, Rice, and Other Flours

The above flours, plus potato, oat, barley, and soy flour, as well as various meals, are some other common flours that are often used in baking. Each adds a different variety of flavor, character, texture, and appearance to your bread. They are fun and easy to work with. If you, or someone in your family, is restricted to nongluten foods, you *might* be able to use some of these flours, since several have little or no gluten content. There are a few gluten-free recipes in this book to give you an idea or two.

Unbleached, Enriched White Flour

White flour is a mixture of hard wheat, soft wheat, barley flour, thiamine, riboflavin, iron, and niacin. The bran and the wheat germ have been removed to prevent spoilage, but since they provide the vast majority of the nutritional value in flour, the government requires the industry to enrich the flour. Of the twenty-one different vitamins and minerals contained in whole grain flour that are lost in processing, white flour is enriched with four of the least expensive, synthetically produced vitamins. When you must use unbleached flour, please add one tablespoon of soy flour for every cup of unbleached flour. It will greatly improve the nutritional value of your bread by raising the protein level.

Wheat Germ

The germ is the living part of a grain of wheat. It's the spark of life that grows when the wheat is planted. The germ is very high in vitamins and is a natural source of vitamin E. If you add wheat germ to your dough, always bake it the same day. Otherwise, the wheat germ will digest the dough and the watery mess left over will not be bakeable.

Pellet Yeast

Pellet yeast is available in some grocery stores and in many health food stores. It is made for commercial use and is much stronger and fresher than the by-the-packet sort, as well as half the cost. You don't use it up as quickly either, since two teaspoons of pellet yeast equal one tablespoon of processed yeast. Use one level teaspoon of pellet yeast for every cup of liquid in the recipe; remember that liquid includes oil, eggs, honey, molasses, cottage cheese, or any other moist ingredient. This yeast is very strong, so try not to use more than four to five teaspoons per recipe. Always dissolve it in warm water or another liquid before using it. If your yeast is old and you don't know whether it's still usable, try this simple test. In a measuring cup, mix together ½ cup of warm water, a tablespoon of your yeast, and a teaspoon of honey or molasses. Let the mixture stand fifteen minutes. If there isn't at least ½ inch of foam in the cup by that time, buy fresher yeast.

Sea Salt

Because it comes from the sea rather than being mined from the earth, sea salt contains many trace elements that do not occur in earth salt. Sea salt does not contain additives that guard against lumping, but a few grains of rice in your salt shaker will take care of that! Use half as much sea salt as table salt in a recipe.

Kelp Powder

Kelp powder is a great saltlike product and may be substituted in place of table salt in any recipe, in the same proportions. Low in sodium, it is ideal for restricted diets and is a great natural source of iodine and other elements. Kelp won't turn food green or make it taste weird; it just gives food a salty flavor. However, yeast bread made with kelp powder will not rise so quickly and completely as bread made with salt.

Pure Oils

Oils that are made without using high heat and chemicals are said to be pure oils. Cold-pressing preserves a greater amount of vitamins and provides a more natural product. High in polyunsaturates and known to aid in the reduction of cholesterol levels, soybean, safflower, sunflower, sesame, peanut, and other oils are of high nutritional value.

Raw Honey

Honey extracted without the use of heat is said to be raw. In baking, use half as much honey as the sugar called for in the recipe, and compensate for the honey's extra liquid by lowering another liquid in the recipe. One cup sugar equals ½ cup honey minus ¼ cup of liquid.

Raw Sugar

There are many sorts of sugar on the market and all of them are processed in one way or another. White sugar is unacceptable; brown sugar is white sugar sprayed with molasses, so it isn't much better. The refined sugar substitutes are even worse. There are also the so-called raw sugars, most of which are raw only in their appearance or in their packaging. Only one truly raw sugar is on the market at this time. It comes from Nicaragua and I recommend it. It is a raw cane syrup from which only debris have been removed. It is high in minerals, and because the carbohydrate is unrefined, the body can digest it more slowly and more naturally. When using Nicaraguan raw sugar, use just slightly less than if you were using brown sugar. It may be hard and lumpy occasionally, so break it up in your blender, a little at a time.

Blackstrap Molasses

The iron-rich leftover of the sugar refining process, molasses is making a comeback as a sweetener. Full, flavorful, and nutrition-laden, blackstrap molasses is ideal for all baking. Use about half as much molasses as sugar in a recipe and remember to compensate for the liquid added by reducing another liquid in the recipe. Use extra molasses to taste, if you wish. Other uses for molasses include adding it to brown gravies, soups, and baked bean dishes.

Diastatic Malt (Barley Malt Sweetener)

Diastatic malt may be used in place of other sweeteners to feed the yeast in your dough. Only one teaspoon per loaf will give you bread that is bigger, tastier, and more finely textured than usual. It is sold commercially in natural food stores, but you may wish to make it yourself. It's not difficult and it will really add extra pizzazz to your bread!

Soak one cup of hulled or unhulled barley or wheat berries in four cups of warm water overnight. Drain (reserving the liquid for other baking needs if you wish) and put the swollen kernels in a two-quart jar. Cover with a sprouting lid and store in a warm, dark place for two to three days, rinsing in cool water at least three times per day. When the sprouts are about a half-inch long, dry them in a dehydrator, or in a warm oven with the door ajar. When the sprouts are completely dried, grind them in a blender or food mill. If you wish, you may sift for two grades of malt. You will have about one cup of diastatic malt, enough for at least forty-eight loaves of fine textured and beautiful bread.

Raw Milk and Other Dairy Products

Fresh milk from healthy cows is terrific. Untouched by heat, synthetic vitamins, or an extended stay in the dairy case, fresh raw milk can be the best milk. The taste will tell you which you prefer. Cultured foods such as cheese, yogurt, cottage cheese, kefir, and ice cream are fresher when made from raw milk, and contain all the enzymes and other components that are lost in processed milk. Butter, whether raw or processed, is better than margarine or shortening. I cook exclusively with butter and cold-pressed oils. The little can of shortening I have is for lubricating the vegetable juicer.

Noninstant Powdered Milk

Powdered milk that has not been oxidized is called noninstant. It takes a bit of effort to dissolve it in water, but its nutritional value is higher than the instant crystals. Noninstant powdered milk is a great addition to all breads because it works as a binder. For every cup of fresh milk called for in a recipe, use $^7/_8$ cup of water and ¼ cup of powdered milk. Stir the milk in with the flour, to prevent lumping, before adding them to the other ingredients. Noninstant powdered milk is also the best if you make your own yogurt.

Farm Fresh Eggs

Brown eggs and white eggs laid at the same chicken farm have no nutritional difference. The nutritional value in eggs comes from the chickens' feed. Make sure the chickens are allowed to be on the ground and scratching, and that they are not being forced to lay under artificial lighting. Happy, well-fed, scratching, rested chickens produce better eggs.

Carob Powder

At last, the flavor of chocolate with only half the carbohydrates, none of the caffeine, and lower allergic reactions. Also known as St. John's Bread, carob is becoming widely used and is preferred to chocolate and cocoa products. It contains two percent fat, as opposed to chocolate's fifty-two percent, and has a whole array of vitamins and minerals not evident in cocoa products. It may be substituted for cocoa powder in equal proportions. Three tablespoons of carob powder plus two tablespoons of water may be substituted for one square of baker's chocolate. Use carob to make great brownies, breads, cakes, fudge, candy, or anything else calling for chocolate. You may wish to add extra vanilla and a dash of cloves to enhance the flavor.

Baking Powder (Rumford)

All baking powders on the market are double-acting. The combination of chemicals provides for a leavening action in the bowl, and another in the oven or on the griddle. What we use to secure this action depends on our choice of baking powders. I prefer the Rumford brand because it is lower in sodium than other brands and also contains no alum (which also lowers the sodium content). Use it in baking at the same proportion as other baking powders. Its special ingredients are especially appreciated because they do not leave a metallic aftertaste in the food as their competitors may seem to.

Tapioca Flour

Used in Asian cooking and found most easily in Asian or natural food stores, tapioca flour is an effective thickener. It is not so refined as cornstarch, will not be cloudy in cooking, thickens quickly, and offers no taste of its own. Be careful to mix it with either dry or wet ingredients prior to heating the foods involved. Lack of care on this point will produce incurable lumps.

How To Make Perfect Bread

Breadmaking is so easy. Just knowing a few basics can help you make great bread. The first thing you need to do is to forget your past failures; they simply don't count! Try my no-nonsense way to make great bread—the hints will give you a basic idea of how most recipes act most of the time.

Dissolve the Yeast in Warm Water

How warm is warm? For dissolving yeast, warm is water-to-wash-your-face-with warm, between 105° and 130° Fahrenheit. Add the yeast to the warm water and stir a bit, if you wish. If the water is too cool, the yeast will not dissolve; if it is too hot, the yeast will be killed. When the temperature is right, the yeast should be foaming within ten to fifteen minutes. If it doesn't foam, discard it and begin again. Yeast takes five minutes to dissolve, whether you stir it or not. Personally, I like to leave it alone to watch the bubbling pattern in the bowl. If there is a sweetener in the recipe, add no more than a few tablespoons of it to the mixture and the yeast will work faster.

Let It Stand

If you let the yeast-water-sweetener mixture stand now for fifteen minutes (during which time it will start to foam), you can shorten the rising time later. This gives the yeast a real boost and activates it well. It is also a good way to make sure the yeast is good.

Begin Adding Ingredients

Add about half of the flour, mixed together with any powdered milk, gluten flour, carob powder, or other lumping ingredients. Next, add and stir in the liquids such as the oil, eggs, milk, yogurt, and honey. Only then may you add the salt. (Adding the salt any sooner can kill or weaken the yeast.) Mix well.

Add the Remaining Flour

Every kind of flour soaks up liquid at a different rate, so the amount of the remaining flour may be different for different recipes. Add it slowly, until the dough comes away from the sides of the bowl and begins to form a dough ball, or until it is too difficult for you to stir any longer. There is no magic time here; you decide when to turn the dough onto the board.

Onto the Board

When it is time to turn the dough onto the bread board, sprinkle some flour onto the board. You will want to be more or less generous with the flour, depending on how gooey (such a professional word!) the dough is. Make sure you cover the area you intend to use, leaving no unfloured spots. Turn the dough out onto the floured surface, scraping the bowl and spoon. Sprinkle the top of the dough with a bit more flour, flour your hands, and now . . .

You Knead It

For every person who kneads bread, there is a style of doing it. There are pushers, punchers, smashers, folders, and squeezers; some people even combine several styles with a little elbow action of their own. There is no one right way to do it, although some methods are less messy than others. Basically, what you want to do is to exercise the dough until the gluten becomes elastic. The end result, a smooth and elastic loaf, comes from exercising the gluten until it begins to stretch and hold the dough together in a firm and smooth ball. Kneading normally takes six to ten minutes for a one- or two-loaf recipe. The gluten will develop in that time, so kneading much past that is a waste of energy and arm muscle. Be good to your biceps and the bread will come out just fine. Remember to keep the board and your hands well floured. You may not use all of the flour the recipe calls for, so add it slowly. The dough will absorb it very quickly at first, then it will slow down. If you think it's time to stop adding flour to the board, test the bread by patting it. If it's still sticky, it will take a bit more flour. If you haven't used all the flour in the recipe, it's OK. If you have used a little more than the recipe called for, that's fine, too. As I said, flours absorb at different rates in different recipes, so follow your recipe, but listen to your dough. It will tell you when to stop.

Kneading Hints

Keeping your fingers flat will keep them cleaner. Try not to squish the dough—pushing, pressing, and punching are less messy. Use up the flour on your bread board by "mopping up" with the dough before you add more. Clean up your surface with a pancake turner. If your hands get really messy, take some flour in your hands and rub them together as though you were washing them. The dough will come right off and you can continue kneading without losing any dough.

Let It Rise

One of the reasons people don't make bread is their idea that it must rise several times, which is very time consuming. What they don't realize is that most breads will do just fine if baked after the first rising. The only thing rising does, basically, is improve the texture of the bread, so if you are short of time, skip to the next step. If you do have time, then go ahead and let it rise once or twice before putting it in the pan. Place the dough in an oiled bowl, turn the dough to oil it well, and cover the bowl with a dry cloth towel; set it in a warm place until the dough has doubled in bulk. With your fist, punch the dough back down to its original size. Turn it over and let it rise again, if you wish, then punch it down again.

Rising in the Pan

The shape of the bread is determined by the pan used, so choose what you wish: traditional loaf, mini-loaf, round, flat, bundt, or what have you. Oil the pan well, then oil your hands. Pick up the dough and shape it until it is smooth on top. Tuck any folds or imperfections underneath; they will bake out and no one will know they were there. Place the dough in the pan, smooth side down. Press it into the pan, then turn it smooth side up. (This step oils and shapes the top of the loaf.) Cover the pan with a dry cloth towel and let it rise in a warm place until the dough doubles in bulk. Let it rise once or let it rise several times; it will taste great either way.

The Final Steps

Bake the bread in a preheated oven until it's done. (Done bread sounds hollow when tapped on the top.) Remove it from the oven and let it cool in the pan for about five minutes, then shake it out of the pan. Let it finish cooling on its side on a wire rack. If you want a crispy crust, do nothing. If you prefer a softer crust, then brush a bit of oil or butter onto it when it comes out of the oven and it will be perfect for easy cutting. Cool the loaf completely before storing it, if it lasts that long. The bread may be stored in the refrigerator or frozen. Either way, the ice is broken—you have made bread. A few more tricks, then on to the treats!

Special Tips

Let the dough rise only until doubled. It is always tempting to let it rise just a bit more because it will look so beautiful. Well, the chances are it will fall and look more like a skateboard, so only until doubled, please. Dough may also fall if too much yeast is used. Extra yeast does make the dough rise faster, but it could fall, so don't be tempted by that idea either.

If your bread is crumbly, it may need a bit more kneading and also may need a bit of gluten added. Add no more than two teaspoons per cup of flour in the recipe.

Beware of your oven. It may heat unevenly, which could cause an overdone top or bottom, or cause your bread to be toasty on the outside and raw on the inside. This could be because the thermostat is irregular or the temperature in the recipe from another book is too hot or you forgot to preheat your oven before putting the bread in.

Be creative. Remember that it's easy to make your bread in shapes other than loaves. You can make your own hamburger and hot dog buns, dinner rolls, bread sticks, or pretzels; you can also braid the dough the same way you braid hair. You can also invent your own breads very easily. One loaf of bread has about 1½ to 2 cups of liquid total, including oil, eggs, honey, molasses, milk, juice, and water. That means about 1½ to 2 teaspoons of yeast and about 4 to 6 cups of flour. Decide which flavor you wish to be predominant, remember the liquid-yeast-solids ratio you need for the number of loaves you plan to make (write it all down as you go along), knead well, bake, and enjoy. For more coarsely textured bread and extra whole grain goodness, add a cup of cereal to your recipe instead of a cup of flour. Try different combinations for seven-, ten-, or even fourteen-grain breads. Add sprouted wheat to give your bread a classic "wheat berry" flavor. A little natural rum or almond or citrus flavoring can be very tasty.

You may also vary recipes by adding herbs like parsley, chives, thyme, or sage. Onions, mushrooms, cheese, or currants may also be added in ¼- to ½-cup total quantities without causing a problem. Many kinds of chopped nuts or fruits make delicious additions, as do sesame seeds, poppy seeds, or other goodies sprinkled over the dough before baking. You may also glaze the bread with egg, water, milk, or honey; glazing before baking makes a crisp crust, glazing after baking makes a soft crust.

In any case, bread is beautiful, and whoever takes the time to make bread is a super person. If it doesn't work out at first, just keep trying and it will soon be perfect. Ignore anyone who gives you a bad time. Love and food have gone together in our culture since warm kitchens and hot cookies after school. You are special because you are making bread, and there's a little bit of love in every loaf of bread.

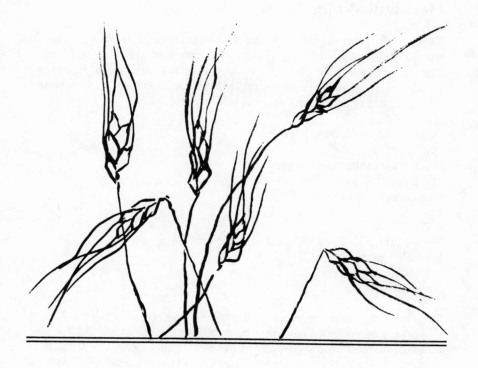

Yeast Breads, Muffins, and Rolls

Healthful White Bread

This is my favorite white bread recipe because it is so effective in teaching resistant tastebuds about the wonders of whole wheat bread. My trick with this recipe is to slowly replace the unbleached flour with whole wheat flour over a period of several months, so your family comes to appreciate the taste of delicious whole grain bread.

Pellet yeast   1½ teaspoons
Warm water   ½ cup
Blackstrap molasses   1 teaspoon
Unbleached flour   1 cup
Raw honey   2 tablespoons
Eggs   2
Oil   ½ cup
Noninstant powdered milk   2 tablespoons
Sea salt   ½ teaspoon
Whole wheat flour   1 cup
Unbleached flour   1¼ cups

Dissolve yeast in warm water and molasses; let rest 10 minutes. Mix in the next 6 ingredients; set aside to bubble for 10 minutes. Add whole wheat flour and beat vigorously. On counter surface, make a patch of remaining unbleached flour; set dough in center. Knead, first with a spoon, then with floured hands, pressing and rolling dough around to gather all the flour. When dough is smooth and elastic, place in oiled, standard 8-inch loaf pan, cover with a towel, and let rise in a warm place until doubled in bulk. Bake at 350° for 35 minutes. Cool in pan for 5 minutes, then remove and cool on side on a wire rack.

Honey-Wheat Bread

This heavy, solid bread is made by the sponge method, which is a more traditional form of allowing the yeast to grow than I normally suggest, similar to the sourdough method in its bubbling action. It develops the gluten in the flour more completely than with the faster method and provides a stronger base for the yeast. The sponge method is an acceptable technique if you have time to devote to it.

Pellet yeast   2 teaspoons
Raw honey   1 teaspoon
Warm water   ½ cup
Whole wheat flour   1 cup
Sea salt   ½ teaspoon
Whole wheat flour   3 cups
Raw honey   ¼ cup
Egg   1
Oil   ¼ cup
Skim milk   ½ cup, warm
Whole wheat flour   2 tablespoons

Dissolve yeast and honey in warm water; let mixture bubble several minutes. Add 1 cup flour and salt, and mix well. Let mixture stand 20 minutes to form the sponge. Add next 5 ingredients to sponge and blend thoroughly. Oil your hands and squeeze dough until it forms a ball. Knead in remaining 2 tablespoons of flour for about 5 minutes, then slam dough down hard on counter several times. (This is called the Italian shock treatment; it works to develop the gluten very quickly.) In a warm place, let dough rise in an oiled, standard 8-inch loaf pan until doubled in bulk, then bake at 350° for 60 minutes, or until done. Cool in pan for 5 minutes, then remove and cool loaf on its side on wire rack; store overnight before slicing thinly.

Six Whole Wheat Loaves

A favorite customer gave me this recipe for lots of bread. It's great for the serious baker with many mouths to feed or for the busy baker with only so much time to make enough for several weeks.

Pellet yeast   3 tablespoons
Raw honey   1 tablespoon
Warm water   ¾ cup
Oil   1 cup
Sea salt   5 teaspoons
Raw honey   1 cup
Warm water   7½ cups
Whole wheat flour   17 to 19 cups

Dissolve yeast and 1 tablespoon honey in ¾ cup warm water; let bubble 10 minutes. Add oil, salt, remaining honey, remaining warm water, and 8 cups of flour; mix very well. Work in remaining flour until dough leaves the sides of the bowl, then turn onto a floured surface and knead until dough is smooth and elastic. Shape into 6 loaves and place in 6 oiled, standard 8-inch loaf pans. Cover loaves with a towel and let rise in a warm place until doubled in bulk, then bake at 350° for 35 to 40 minutes. Place loaves on their sides on a wire rack to cool.
Note: If you brush the tops of the loaves with butter when they come out of the oven, they will be easier to slice later.

"Seattle Today's" Whole Wheat Bread

Thanks to my friends Shirley Hudson and Cliff Lenz of KING TV's "Seattle Today Show," this simple and delicious bread is still requested by many people. It is basic, a great one to learn with, and yummy.

Pellet yeast 2 scant teaspoons
Warm water 1¾ cups
Blackstrap molasses 1 tablespoon
Noninstant powdered milk 2 tablespoons
Oil 1 tablespoon
Orange peel 1 teaspoon grated
Sea salt ½ teaspoon
Whole wheat flour 4 to 4½ cups, plus as needed

Dissolve yeast in warm water, add molasses, and let mixture bubble for 10 minutes. Mix in powdered milk, oil, orange peel, and salt. Gradually add flour until dough pulls away from the sides of the bowl. Turn out on a floured surface and knead for 5 to 7 minutes, making dough smooth and elastic; add more flour as needed to keep dough from sticking to your hands. Place dough in an oiled, standard 8-inch loaf pan, or shape as you choose, and let it rise, covered, in a warm place until doubled in bulk. Bake at 350° for 40 to 45 minutes, or until bread sounds hollow when tapped. Remove from pan and cool on its side on a wire rack.

Farmhouse Cracked Wheat Bread

Cracked wheat   2½ cups
Boiling water   2 cups
Noninstant powdered milk   1 cup
Raw honey   ¼ cup
Blackstrap molasses   ¼ cup
Safflower oil   ¼ cup
Sea salt   5 teaspoons
Pellet yeast   2 tablespoons
Warm water   4 cups
Whole wheat flour   5 cups
Unbleached flour   up to 10 cups
Soy flour   6 tablespoons

Soak cracked wheat in boiling water for 30 minutes; add powdered milk and stir well. Mix in honey, molasses, oil, and salt; set aside. Dissolve yeast in 1 cup warm water, set aside 10 minutes, then add to cracked wheat mixture along with remaining warm water. Slowly add the whole wheat flour, 1 cup at a time; stir well after each addition. Add the soy flour and enough unbleached flour to make a stiff dough, turn out onto floured surface, and knead until dough is smooth and elastic. Place dough in buttered bowl, cover with a towel, and allow to rise in a warm place until doubled in bulk. Punch dough down and shape it into 4 loaves. Place in oiled, standard 8-inch loaf pans and let rise until doubled in bulk. Bake at 450° for 10 minutes, then reduce temperature to 350° and bake 30 minutes more. The loaves are done if they sound hollow when tapped. Remove from pans and cool loaves on sides on a wire rack.

Wheat Germ Bread

Warm water 1½ cups
Oil 6 tablespoons
Raw honey ½ cup
Sea salt ¼ teaspoon
Pellet yeast 1 tablespoon
Warm water ½ cup
Eggs 2
Wheat germ 1 cup
Whole wheat flour 2 cups
Unbleached flour 2½ cups
Soft butter for brushing

Combine 1½ cups warm water, oil, honey, and salt; set aside. Dissolve yeast in remaining warm water; let stand 10 minutes. Combine yeast and honey mixtures, add eggs and wheat germ, and beat for 2 minutes. Slowly add whole wheat flour, beat again, and slowly add unbleached flour; dough will be sticky. Spread dough evenly into 2 oiled, standard 8-inch pans and pat the tops of the loaves with floured hands to shape. Let rise, covered, in a warm place until almost doubled in bulk, then bake at 375° for 45 minutes. Remove from pans, brush the tops of the baked loaves with butter, and cool on their sides on a wire rack.
Note: Do not make this dough in advance and store in the refrigerator. Wheat germ is very much alive, and the bread must be made and baked promptly. It is particularly delicious as breakfast toast.

Basic Sourdough Bread

Sourdough baking is fun, easy, and part of the Northwest's heritage. During the Alaska gold rush, sourdough was such a valuable part of the miners' diet that people were killed for stealing someone else's starter. The only peril now seems to be with making sure you're out of the way when the bread comes out of the oven.

Sourdough starter   1 recipe less 1 cup
Raw honey or blackstrap molasses   3 tablespoons
Sea salt   1 teaspoon
Milk or water   1 cup
Whole wheat, rye, unbleached, or other flour   6 to 7½ cups,
    plus as needed
Cornmeal   for sprinkling
Cream or oil   for brushing (optional)

Combine starter, honey, salt, milk, and 3 cups of flour; mix thoroughly. Slowly add remaining flour until dough comes away from the sides of the bowl, then turn onto a floured surface and knead until smooth and elastic. Let dough rest 10 minutes, then knead again, adding more flour as needed. Shape into 2 loaves and place on cornmeal-sprinkled cookie sheets or pie tins. Cover dough with a towel and let rise in a warm place until doubled in bulk, then brush tops with cream for a shiny crust. Can slash tops—either crisscross or vertical—with a razor blade to ½-inch thickness. Bake at 375° for 40 minutes, then cool loaves on their sides on a wire rack.
Note: This basic recipe lends itself well to experimenting. Create and enjoy!

Sourdough Starter

The starter will keep fairly well for several weeks between uses, so don't be frightened away from leaving it in the refrigerator for awhile. Someone will remind you it's there.

Pellet yeast ½ teaspoon
Warm water ⅓ cup
Whole wheat, rye, unbleached, or other flour ¾ cup

Make the primary starter by dissolving yeast in warm water. Add ¾ cup of flour; mix well. Cover loosely and set aside several hours; mixture should be light and fluffy. Place in a container that will allow for doubling and store in refrigerator for at least 24 to 48 hours before using the first time. After adding to the starter, allow it to rest overnight before using it.

Whole wheat, rye, unbleached, or other flour 4 cups
Warm water 2½ cups

At least 10 hours before you want to make bread, combine the primary starter with 4 cups of flour and 2½ cups of warm water. Mix well, cover, and set aside 8 hours, or until ready to use. This is the Sourdough Starter. Before using, put 1 cup of starter back in primary starter container; return to refrigerator to use as primary starter for future baking. You must repeat this last step to turn it into Sourdough Starter again.

Special Dinner Rye Bread

Warm water   ½ cup
Caraway seeds   2 teaspoons
Raw honey   ½ teaspoon
Pellet yeast   1½ teaspoons
Apple cider vinegar   ¼ cup
Rye flour   ½ cup
Unbleached flour   ¾ cup
Whole wheat flour   ½ cup
Sea salt   ½ teaspoon
Unbleached flour   ½ cup
Oil   for brushing
Orange peel   1 teaspoon grated (optional)

Mix together the warm water, caraway seeds, honey, and yeast; let stand 10 minutes. Add next 5 ingredients and stir well. Place ¼ cup of remaining unbleached flour on your kneading surface and knead dough into it for 5 minutes. Slowly add the remaining ¼ cup of unbleached flour, blending in well with your fingers. Slam dough onto counter 10 times, hard. Roll it around, shaping it with your hands. Place shaped loaf in an oiled, standard 8-inch loaf pan, cover with a towel, and let rise in a warm place until doubled in bulk. Bake at 350° for 30 minutes, then remove from oven and brush oil over top; sprinkle with orange peel, return to oven, and bake 20 to 25 minutes more. Remove from oven and serve immediately, or cool on its side on a wire rack.
Note: This is an especially delicious dinner bread and will go with most meals.

Swedish Rye Bread

Swedish rye is characterized by the use of orange juice or orange peel.

Pellet yeast 1 tablespoon
Raw honey ¾ cup
Warm water 1 cup
Gluten flour ¼ cup
Rye flour 2 cups
Orange juice 2 cups, warm
Oil ¼ cup
Sea salt 1 heaping teaspoon
Whole wheat flour 6 cups

Dissolve the yeast and honey in warm water; set aside 5 minutes. Mix gluten flour and rye flour; add to yeast mixture along with orange juice and oil. Add salt and 3 cups whole wheat flour; beat 100 strokes or more to develop the texture and the gluten. Let dough rest 5 minutes, then slowly add enough of remaining whole wheat flour to make a stiff dough; turn out and knead dough on a floured surface until smooth, elastic, and no longer sticky. Shape into 2 round or long loaves, place in oiled pans, and let rise, covered, in a warm place until doubled in bulk. Bake at 350° for 40 to 50 minutes. Loaves are easier to cut when cooled for 15 minutes before serving.

Variations: If you prefer traditional dark rye bread, substitute blackstrap molasses for the honey. If you wish to make this bread lighter, substitute unbleached flour for ½ the whole wheat flour. This bread may also be shaped into long, skinny "deli" loaves; bake in an oiled glass bread tube, oiled French bread pan, or on oiled cookie sheet.

Very Scandinavian Rye Bread

Water   1 cup
Blackstrap molasses   ½ cup
Orange peel   of 5 to 6 oranges, grated
Caraway seeds   2 tablespoons crushed
Fennel seeds   2 tablespoons crushed
Butter   1 tablespoon
Sea salt   1½ teaspoons
Buttermilk   2 cups
Baking soda   ½ teaspoon
Pellet yeast   2 tablespoons
Raw honey   1 teaspoon
Warm water   ¼ cup
Rye flour   4 cups
Whole wheat flour   3 cups, plus as needed
Blackstrap molasses   ⅛ cup
Water   ⅛ cup

In a saucepan, heat together first 7 ingredients until butter is melted; set aside to cool. In a bowl, mix together buttermilk and baking soda; stir into molasses mixture. Dissolve yeast and honey in warm water and let mixture bubble for 10 minutes; add to the now lukewarm molasses mixture. Slowly add the rye flour and mix very well. Slowly add the whole wheat flour, but only enough to make a soft but firm dough. Turn out onto a floured surface and knead until smooth and no longer sticky, adding extra flour as needed. Let the dough rest 5 minutes, then knead it 10 minutes more. Place in oiled bowl, cover with a towel, and let rise in a warm place until doubled in bulk. Punch dough down, then shape into 3 round loaves and place in oiled pans. With a knife or razor blade, slash an X, about ½ inch deep, across the top of each loaf. Cover loaves and let rise in a warm place until doubled in bulk, then bake at 375° for 35 to 40 minutes. Combine molasses and water; brush over the baked bread and cool on a wire rack.
Note: This bread can be thinly sliced and used as a base for traditional open-faced sandwiches, but it's also delicious served in hunks with a hearty soup or with cheese and sliced apples.

Black Peasant Bread

Pellet yeast 5 teaspoons
Warm water ½ cup
Raw honey 1 tablespoon
Water 2 cups
Apple cider vinegar ¼ cup
Blackstrap molasses ¼ cup
Butter ¼ cup
Rye flour 4 cups
Bran 2 cups
Caraway seeds 2 tablespoons crushed
Carob powder 3 tablespoons
Instant coffee or mocha flavoring 2 teaspoons
Dried chives 2 teaspoons
Fennel ½ teaspoon crushed
Sea salt 1 tablespoon
Whole wheat flour for flouring kneading surface
Egg yolk 1 (optional)
Water 1 tablespoon (optional)

Dissolve yeast in warm water, stir in honey, and let stand 10 minutes. In a saucepan, heat together water, vinegar, molasses, and butter until butter is melted; cool to lukewarm. Add next 8 ingredients to yeast mixture and mix well. Add cooled molasses mixture and beat until stiff. Turn dough out onto a surface floured with whole wheat flour and knead for 15 minutes, adding more whole wheat flour to keep dough from sticking. Place in buttered bowl, cover with a towel, and let rise in a warm place until doubled in bulk. Punch dough down, shape into 2 round or long loaves, and let rise in oiled pans. Beat egg yolk with water and brush on bread for shiny crusts. Bake at 350° for 50 minutes. Cool before slicing or serve hot if pieces are to be torn off.

Pumpernickel

Pellet yeast   2 teaspoons
Warm water   1½ cups
Blackstrap molasses   1 cup
Caraway seeds   2 tablespoons
Sea salt   1½ teaspoons
Oil   3 tablespoons
Rye flour   2 cups
Whole wheat flour   4 cups

Dissolve yeast in warm water; let stand 5 minutes. Add next 5 ingredients and mix 5 minutes. Gradually add whole wheat flour, beating well. When all the flour has been added, turn dough onto a floured surface and knead until smooth, elastic, and no longer sticky. Place dough in an oiled bowl, cover with a towel and let it rise in a warm place for 30 minutes. Punch dough down, knead for 1 minute, then let it rest for 10 minutes. Shape into a round or long loaf and place in an oiled pan; cover, put in a warm place, and let rise until doubled in bulk. Bake at 450° for 15 minutes, then reduce heat to 350° and bake 30 minutes more. Cool on a wire rack before serving.
Note: This is wonderful served with a mild white cheese, sliced apples, and the sparkling beverage of your choice.

Finnish Pumpernickel

Pellet yeast   2 teaspoons
Potato water*   1¼ cups, lukewarm
Rye flour or rye meal   1 cup
Whole wheat flour   1½ cups, plus as needed
Butter   1 tablespoon, melted
Sea salt   1 teaspoon
Rye flour or rye meal   ½ cup

Dissolve yeast in warm potato water and let stand for 10 minutes. Add 1 cup rye flour and beat for 1 minute. Cover and set aside 15 minutes, then add whole wheat flour, butter, and salt; beat 1 minute, adding a bit more wheat flour, if necessary, to make a soft dough. Turn onto a surface that has been sprinkled with remaining ½ cup rye flour, cover dough with a bowl, and let stand for 10 minutes. Knead in rye flour until dough is smooth and resilient, then shape into a round loaf, place in an oiled pie pan, and let rise, covered, in a warm place until doubled in bulk. Prick loaf with a fork all over the top and bake at 375° for 45 minutes. Cool, then slice very thin in traditional fashion.

* Boil potatoes; reserve cooking water to use as potato water.

Country Farina Bread

Dark farina is a special product of our old mill. It is farina the way it used to be: made from the whole grain, freshly ground, hearty, flavorful, and packed with country goodness. Add it to your bread for a slightly coarser texture and a more robust flavor.

Milk   3 cups, scalded
Raw honey   3 tablespoons
Sea salt   ½ teaspoon
Oil   ¼ cup
Pellet yeast   1 tablespoon
Warm water   ¼ cup
Dark farina   3 cups
Lemon peel   1 teaspoon grated (optional)
Walnuts   ½ cup chopped (optional)
Vanilla   1 teaspoon (optional) or
     Powdered vanilla   ½ teaspoon (optional)
Whole wheat flour   5 cups

Combine milk, honey, salt, and oil; cool to lukewarm. Dissolve yeast in warm water, then add to lukewarm milk mixture. Add farina, lemon peel, walnuts, and vanilla; beat 50 strokes, then let mixture rest 5 minutes. Add 4 cups of whole wheat flour and stir well; cover with a towel and let rise in a warm place for 1 hour. Knead in enough of remaining wheat flour to make dough smooth and elastic. Shape into 2 loaves, and place in oiled, standard 8-inch loaf pans; cover with a towel and let rise until doubled in bulk. Bake at 350° for 1 hour, or until done. Cool before slicing.

Gluten-Free Rice Bread

Many people are allergic to gluten, the part of the wheat that makes bread rise and hold together. The texture of this gluten-free bread is similar to banana bread.

Pellet yeast 1 tablespoon
Raw honey ¼ cup
Warm water 3 cups, plus as needed
Brown rice flour 6 cups
Oil ¼ cup
Sea salt 1 tablespoon
Honey or jam for spreading (optional)

Dissolve yeast and honey in warm water; set aside 15 minutes. Add flour, oil, and salt and mix well, adding a bit more warm water to make a soft dough. Stir well and fill 2 oiled, standard 8-inch loaf pans ¾ full. Cover, put in a warm place, and let stand 45 minutes. Bake at 350° for 30 minutes for 2 small loaves; bread will be crusty and cracked on top. Serve warm with honey.
Variation: Roll out dough to ¾-inch thickness and cut into 2-inch muffin rounds; let rise on oiled cookie sheets. Bake at 350° for 20 to 25 minutes. Makes 24 muffins.

Braided Soy Bread

Pellet yeast 1½ teaspoons
Blackstrap molasses 1 tablespoon
Warm water 1¾ cups
Gluten flour 2 tablespoons
Whole wheat flour 2 cups
Soy flour 1 cup
Sea salt ½ teaspoon
Whole wheat flour 2 cups
Egg 1
Water scant ¼ cup
Sesame seeds to taste

Dissolve yeast in molasses and warm water; let bubble 10 minutes. Stir gluten flour into 2 cups of whole wheat flour; add to yeast mixture along with soy flour and salt, and stir well. Gradually add enough of the remaining whole wheat flour to form a stiff dough. Turn onto a floured surface and knead for 5 to 7 minutes, or until smooth and resilient. Divide dough into 3 equal parts and roll out each into 12-inch-long "snakes." Join them at 1 end by squishing them firmly together, then braid; transfer braid to oiled cookie sheet or loaf pan. Beat egg and water together and brush onto bread. Sprinkle with sesame seeds, then allow dough to rise in a warm place until doubled in bulk. Bake at 325° for 20 minutes, then continue baking but check every 5 minutes until golden brown and done. Cool and store, or serve hot.

Triticale Buttermilk Bread

Triticale is a wheat and rye hybrid. These two grains have been inter-pollinating for centuries, the first records dating back to early Roman times. It is the only known hybrid grain that is fertile itself and initiates the hybrid on its own. Modern science has been applied to the hybridizing, with the result that triticale is stronger than either wheat or rye, more disease resistant, and has a higher protein content than either. It tastes hearty, favoring the wheat family more than the rye.

Pellet yeast 2 teaspoons
Raw honey 2 tablespoons
Warm water ½ cup
Buttermilk 2 cups, warm
Butter 2 tablespoons
Sea salt 2 teaspoons
Kelp powder ½ teaspoon
Eggs 2
Unbleached flour 1½ cups
Soy flour 2 tablespoons
Baking soda 1 teaspoon
Triticale flour 4 to 5 cups

Dissolve the yeast and honey in warm water; let stand 10 minutes. Add next 8 ingredients and mix well. Slowly add enough triticale flour to form a stiff dough. Turn out onto a floured surface and knead until dough is smooth, elastic, and no longer sticky. Place dough in an oiled bowl, cover with a cloth towel, and let rise in a warm place until doubled in bulk. Punch down and knead slightly, then shape into 2 loaves and place in oiled, standard 8-inch loaf pans; cover with a towel and let rise in a warm place until doubled in bulk. Bake at 375° for 40 to 45 minutes; cool loaves on their sides on a wire rack.

Early Colonial Bread

Coarse cornmeal   ½ cup
Raw honey   ⅓ cup
Sea salt   1 tablespoon
Boiling water   2 cups
Oil   ¼ cup
Pellet yeast   2 teaspoons
Warm water   ½ cup
Whole wheat flour   ¾ cup
Rye flour   ½ cup
Unbleached flour   4 to 4½ cups

Combine the first 5 ingredients; cool to lukewarm. Dissolve yeast in warm water, then add to cornmeal mixture. Add whole wheat and rye flours; mix well. Slowly add the unbleached flour until dough is fairly stiff, then turn out onto a floured surface and knead until smooth and elastic. Place in an oiled bowl, cover with a towel, and let rise in a warm place until doubled in bulk. Punch down, shape into 1 large loaf, and place in an oiled 8- or 9-inch loaf pan. Cover with a towel and let loaves rise in a warm place until doubled in bulk, then bake at 350° for 35 to 40 minutes.
Note: This bread is especially good with a hearty meal in the winter, or with a tasty stew and cheese.

Four-Grain Bread

Pellet yeast   1 tablespoon
Warm water   4 cups
Oil   ½ cup
Raw honey   1½ cups
Four-grain cereal   3 cups
Noninstant powdered milk   3 tablespoons
Sea salt   1½ tablespoons
Whole wheat flour   4 cups
Unbleached flour   6 cups

Dissolve yeast in warm water; set aside 10 minutes. Add oil and honey; let mixture stand 10 minutes more. Stir in cereal, powdered milk, salt, and whole wheat flour, and mix very well. Slowly add unbleached flour, 1 cup at a time. Turn out onto a floured surface and knead until dough is no longer sticky; oil hands and continue kneading another 3 minutes. Place dough in an oiled bowl, cover with a towel, and let rise in a warm place until doubled in bulk. Knead dough for 5 minutes more, then divide into 3 loaves and place in 3 oiled, standard 8-inch loaf pans; cover with a towel and let rise in a warm place until doubled in bulk. Bake at 325° for 50 minutes, then cool loaves on sides on wire racks.

Note: This bread will be very smooth if *all* the kneading instructions are followed. For a more hearty texture, knead, place in pans, and allow to rise only once before baking.

Sharon's Bread

Sharon Portin's bread was invented on the air at Cablevision Channel 3 in Lynnwood, Washington, in May 1976. We did several cooking demonstrations for her weekly TV show, and usually the ideas were mine. One day, I surprised her with a box of ingredients and a blank piece of paper; this is what she invented.

Pellet yeast 2 slightly heaping teaspoons
Warm water 1¾ cups
Raw honey ¼ cup
Blackstrap molasses 1 tablespoon
Egg 1
Wheat germ 2 tablespoons
Buckwheat flour ½ cup
Oil 2 tablespoons
Soy flour 2 tablespoons
Sea salt ½ teaspoon
Currants ½ cup
Whole wheat flour 4½ cups
Honey Butter (see Index) for spreading (optional)

Mix together the yeast, water, honey, and molasses; set aside to bubble. Add the next 7 ingredients and mix well. Slowly add the whole wheat flour, stirring rapidly until dough is very stiff. Turn out onto a floured surface and knead until smooth and elastic. Place in oiled, standard 8-inch loaf pan and let rise, covered, in a warm place until doubled in bulk. Bake at 350° for 50 minutes. Cool on a wire rack, then serve, dripping with Honey Butter.

Old Country Bread

This great recipe for "kitchen bread" (whatever is in the kitchen goes into the bread) reflects great ingenuity in using bits of this and that to create rich-tasting and nutritious bread.

Four flaked-grain cereal*   1 cup
Noninstant powdered milk   1 cup
Boiling water   2½ cups
Pellet yeast   2½ teaspoons
Warm water   ½ cup
Oil   3 tablespoons
Blackstrap molasses   ½ cup
Sea salt   2 teaspoons
Soy flour   ½ cup
Millet flour   ½ cup
Barley flour   ¼ cup
Brewer's yeast   ¼ cup
Whole wheat flour   2½ cups
Unbleached flour   3 to 4 cups

Mix together the oats, powdered milk, and boiling water; cool to lukewarm. In another bowl, dissolve pellet yeast in warm water; add to oat mixture along with the next 8 ingredients, and stir well. Slowly add enough unbleached flour to form a stiff dough that leaves the sides of the bowl. Turn out onto a floured surface and knead until smooth and elastic, adding more flour as needed to keep dough from being sticky. Place in an oiled bowl, cover with a towel, and let rise in a warm place for 30 minutes, then knead lightly and shape into loaves. Place loaves in 2 oiled, standard 8-inch loaf pans, cover with a towel, and let rise in a warm place until doubled in bulk, then bake at 350° for 45 minutes. Cool loaves on their sides on a wire rack.

* Any cereal product that contains rolled oats, rolled wheat, rolled barley, and rolled rye.

Variation: For a shiny crust, glaze before baking with 1 egg white mixed with 1 tablespoon of water.

Super Sour Bread

Over the years, Super Sour Bread has remained the most popular recipe in this book. Small wonder—it tastes terrific!

Flat beer 2 cups
Coarse cornmeal ⅔ cup
Oil 2 tablespoons
Sea salt 1 teaspoon
Blackstrap molasses ½ cup
Warm water ½ cup
Pellet yeast 1 tablespoon
Raw honey 1 tablespoon
Wheat germ ½ cup
Bran ½ cup
Whole wheat flour 2 cups
Gluten flour ¼ cup
Graham flour 1 cup
Unbleached flour 3 cups, or as needed
Egg yolk 1 (optional)
Water 1 tablespoon (optional)

Heat beer to steaming, then stir in cornmeal, oil, salt, and molasses; set aside to cool. Blend together warm water, yeast, and honey; set aside to dissolve. Combine beer and yeast mixtures, then blend in the next 5 ingredients; stir well to develop the texture. Gradually add enough unbleached flour to make a stiff dough. Turn onto a floured surface and knead 10 minutes, adding more unbleached flour as needed to make dough smooth and elastic. Place dough in buttered bowl, cover with a towel, and let rise in a warm place until doubled in bulk. Punch down, shape into 2 loaves, and place in oiled 8- or 9-inch pie pans; cover with a towel and let rise in a warm place until doubled again. Beat together egg yolk and water; brush over tops of loaves, then score; this makes an extra-traditional looking bread. Bake at 375° for 40 minutes. Cool before slicing or serve hot if pieces are to be torn off.
Note: This bread is especially good with a hearty meal, or with cheese and fruit and a fireplace.

Pedersen's Soul Bread

This bread is good for the souls who make it and especially good for the souls who eat it!

Cracked wheat ⅔ cup
Coarse cornmeal ½ cup
Water 1 cup
Light cream ⅔ cup
Milk 1½ cups
Raw honey ½ cup
Sea salt 1 tablespoon
Kelp powder 1 teaspoon
Oil or butter ¼ cup
Blackstrap molasses ¼ cup
Pellet yeast ¼ cup
Warm water ½ cup
Whole wheat flour 3 cups
Soy flour ½ cup
Bran ½ cup
Wheat germ ½ cup
Brewer's yeast ¼ to ½ cup
Unbleached flour up to 6 cups

Soak cracked wheat and cornmeal in water overnight. Next morning, heat together the next 7 ingredients; add to soaked mixture and cool to lukewarm. Dissolve pellet yeast in warm water and add to mixture. Slowly add next 5 ingredients, stirring well. Mix in unbleached flour until dough is stiff enough to knead. Turn out on floured surface and knead for 10 minutes, or until elastic. Place dough in an oiled bowl, cover with a towel, and let rise in a warm place until doubled in bulk. Punch down and shape into 3 loaves. Place in oiled, standard 8-inch loaf pans, cover with a towel, and let rise in a warm place until doubled in bulk, then bake at 350° for 35 to 40 minutes. Cool and slice.

Mark Worstman's Special Bread

My self-assured twelve-year-old son was hanging over my shoulder one Sunday afternoon as I was creating a new bread. He asked me what kind it was, and after I'd evaded him several times, he decided it didn't have a name. His modest suggestion was, of course, to name it after himself. Not wishing to give credit where none was deserved, I said it could be named after him only if he did the kneading. Hoping to get out of it, his instant response was, "But, Mom, I don't know how." He got the same response I did as a little girl: "What a great time to learn!" We put the gooey dough on the floured table, he gave me a blank look, and I said, "Get going." After a few timid pokes and a feeble excuse, he got the hang of it and we had a smooth, elastic dough in no time. A bread was born.

Pellet yeast   2 teaspoons
Warm water   2½ cups
Blackstrap molasses   1 tablespoon
Raw honey   ¼ cup
Soy flour   ½ cup
Gluten flour   ¼ cup
Oat flour   1 cup
Noninstant powdered milk   ¼ cup
Eggs   2
Caraway seeds   1 tablespoon
Sea salt   1 teaspoon
Whole wheat flour   6 to 7 cups

Mix the yeast, water, molasses, and honey together; let rest 15 minutes. Stir together the soy flour, gluten flour, oat flour, and powdered milk; add to yeast mixture along with the eggs, caraway seeds, and salt. Stir in enough whole wheat flour to bring dough away from the sides of the bowl, then place on a floured surface and knead until smooth and elastic. The dough will be a little sticky then, so oil your hands and continue kneading for 5 minutes more. Place dough in an oiled bowl, cover with a towel, and let rise in a warm place until doubled. Punch down, shape into 2 loaves, and place in oiled, standard 8-inch loaf pans; cover with a towel and let rise in a warm place until doubled in bulk. Bake at 350° for 35 to 40 minutes. Cool loaves before slicing.

My Branolabread

Pellet yeast   1 heaping teaspoon
Warm water   ¼ cup
Blackstrap molasses   2 tablespoons
Milk   1 cup, warm
Oil   2 tablespoons
Sea salt   1 teaspoon
Egg   1
Whole wheat flour   1 cup, plus as needed
Graham flour   1 cup
Bran   2 cups

Dissolve yeast in warm water and molasses; wait for mixture to bubble, then add the remaining ingredients and mix well. Turn out onto a floured surface and knead until smooth and elastic; add more whole wheat flour as needed to keep dough from becoming sticky, but remember, bran is very absorbent and drying, so add the flour sparingly. (You may wish to knead with oiled hands at the end if the result is bread too dry for your taste.) Place dough in an oiled, standard 8-inch loaf pan and let rise, covered, in a warm place until doubled in bulk, then bake at 375° for 40 minutes. Cool on wire rack before serving.

Rich Egg Bread

Pellet yeast   1½ teaspoons
Raw honey   2 tablespoons
Warm water   1 cup
Sea salt   ½ teaspoon
Noninstant powdered milk   2 tablespoons
Oil   1 tablespoon
Eggs   3
Whole wheat flour   4 to 5 cups
Cream   for glazing
Sesame seeds   a sprinkle

Dissolve yeast and honey in warm water; set aside for 5 minutes. Stir in the salt, powdered milk, oil, eggs, and 2 cups of flour; mix very well. Gradually add enough of the remaining flour to form a stiff dough. Turn dough out onto a floured surface and knead until smooth and elastic. Place in a buttered bowl, cover with a towel, and let rise in a warm place until doubled in bulk. Shape dough into a loaf or braid, then place in oiled pan. Cover with a towel and let rise in a warm place until doubled, then glaze with cream and sprinkle lightly with sesame seeds. Bake at 350° for 45 minutes. Cool before serving.

Note: This bread is beautifully golden and shiny—just right to show off at a buffet.

Glow-of-Health Bread

Pellet yeast   1 teaspoon
Orange juice   ½ cup, warm
Wheat germ   1 heaping tablespoon
Noninstant powdered milk   1 heaping tablespoon
Soy flour   1 tablespoon
Oil   1 teaspoon
Butter   3 tablespoons
Large egg   1
Blackstrap molasses   1 tablespoon
Sea salt   ½ teaspoon
Pineapple juice   ¼ cup
Unbleached flour   1¼ cups
Whole wheat flour   1¼ cups, plus 2 tablespoons

Dissolve yeast in warm orange juice and let stand 10 minutes. Stir in the next 9 ingredients, then add the unbleached flour and stir well. Stir in ¼ cup of whole wheat flour, then turn dough out and knead in 1 cup of whole wheat flour. When dough becomes sticky, oil your hands and continue kneading several minutes more. Work in the remaining 2 tablespoons of whole wheat flour, shape into a loaf, and place in an oiled, standard 8-inch loaf pan. Put dough in a warm place and let rise, covered, until doubled in bulk. Bake at 350° for 1 hour; eat immediately or cool.

Note: Serve with cheese and fruit for a satisfying meal.

Zesty Cheese Bread

Pellet yeast   2 teaspoons
Warm water   ½ cup
Blackstrap molasses   1 tablespoon
Flat beer   1½ cups
Cheddar cheese   1¾ cups shredded
Butter   2 tablespoons
Whole wheat flour   3 cups
Sea salt   1 teaspoon
Dry mustard   1 teaspoon
Cayenne   a dash
Worcestershire sauce   1 tablespoon
Parsley   1 tablespoon chopped (optional)
Unbleached flour   3 cups

Dissolve the yeast in warm water and molasses. Heat together the beer, cheese, and butter until butter and cheese melt, then cool to lukewarm. Alternately stir in the yeast mixture and the whole wheat flour, beating for 3 minutes. Add the next 5 ingredients, then stir in enough unbleached flour to form a stiff dough. Turn out onto a floured surface and knead 5 to 7 minutes, reflouring the surface as needed to keep the dough from sticking. Shape into 2 loaves or braids; place in oiled pans and let rise, covered, in a warm place until doubled in bulk. Bake at 350° for 45 to 50 minutes. Remove from pans and cool loaves on their sides on a wire rack.
Note: This bread is super with soup and salad.

Special Herb Bread

Pellet yeast   2 teaspoons
Raw honey   1 teaspoon
Warm water   1 cup
Cottage cheese   ⅔ cup
Eggs   2
Oil   2 tablespoons
Sea salt   1 teaspoon
Parsley   1 teaspoon chopped
Dillweed   1 teaspoon chopped
Chives   1 teaspoon chopped
Whole wheat flour   2 cups
Unbleached flour   2 cups

Dissolve yeast and honey in warm water; let bubble for 10 minutes. Add the next 7 ingredients, then stir in the whole wheat flour and beat 3 minutes. Stirring constantly, gradually add enough unbleached flour to form a stiff dough. Turn out onto a floured surface and knead until smooth and elastic; allow dough to rest for 10 minutes, then knead 3 minutes more. Place dough in an oiled bowl, cover with a towel, and let rise in a warm place until doubled. Punch down, shape into a loaf, and place in an oiled 8-inch pie pan. Cover with a towel and let rise in a warm place until doubled, then bake at 350° for 35 to 45 minutes.

Variation: This recipe makes especially good breadsticks. Make long dough "snakes," no more than ½ inch thick and 6 to 8 inches long. Place on an oiled cookie sheet and let rise until doubled. Bake at 400° for 10 minutes, or until crisp. Cool on a wire rack, then enjoy! Makes 2 dozen.

Pocket Bread

Pellet yeast   2 teaspoons
Raw honey   1 tablespoon
Warm water   1¾ cups
Oil   1 tablespoon
Whole wheat flour   2 cups
Sea salt   1 teaspoon
Onion   2 tablespoons minced and sautéed or
     Parsley   2 tablespoons chopped
Whole wheat flour   2 cups
Fine cornmeal   for dusting

Dissolve yeast and honey in warm water; set aside 15 minutes. Add oil and 2 cups of flour; beat vigorously until dough is very elastic. Add salt and onion, then gradually add enough of the remaining flour to make a ball of dough that comes away from the sides of the bowl. Turn out onto a floured surface and knead until smooth and elastic, then let dough rest 10 minutes. Cut dough into 8 mounds about the size of a small tennis ball. Roll out the first 4 until each is as flat as a pancake. Lightly dust a cookie sheet with cornmeal, arrange dough on cookie sheet, and bake at 450° for 8 to 10 minutes, or until bread seems dry; watch carefully to prevent burning. Cool bread on a wire rack while rolling out and baking the remaining dough. When bread is cool, slice in ½ and fill. Makes 8 pocket breads.

Note: Try a filling of sliced cucumbers, chopped tomatoes, shredded lettuce, alfalfa sprouts, finely chopped green onions, and shredded white Cheddar, with yogurt, dillweed and mayonnaise dressing, or make up your own combinations.

Whole Wheat Pizza

Pellet yeast   1 very heaping teaspoon
Warm water   1½ cups
Blackstrap molasses   1 tablespoon
Whole wheat flour   3 cups, plus as needed or
    Whole wheat flour   2 cups and
    Unbleached flour   1 cup
Noninstant powdered milk   2 tablespoons
Sea salt   ½ teaspoon
Tomato sauce, grated cheese, and toppings   to taste

Dissolve yeast in warm water together with molasses; set aside 15 minutes to bubble. Stir in flour, powdered milk, and salt; whip dough with fork until very elastic. Cover and let dough rest in a warm place for 20 minutes, then stir with fork, adding a bit more flour if dough appears too wet. Oil two 13-inch pizza pans and your hands. Divide the dough in ½ and pat out with your hands to cover pans; the best method is to pat a little, let the dough rest, and pat some more. Make sure the dough is spread out evenly, then cover with pizza fixings and bake at 400° for 20 minutes. Enough for 2 pizzas.
Variation: Try a Dessert Pizza. Make a pizza sauce of 8 ounces lemon-flavored yogurt, 1 cup chopped dates, and ½ cup shredded coconut; spread over dough. Arrange 1 cup crushed and drained pineapple, 1 cup apricots, and 1 small can (drained) mandarin oranges on top. Sprinkle with ½ cup walnuts, ½ cup currants, and 2 cups shredded fruity cheese, such as Norwegian Swiss or Finnish Turanmaa; bake at 400° for 20 minutes. This is a terrific dessert and a conversation piece, too! Serve with sparkling cider for a midnight buffet.

Pretzels

This is an authentic kosher recipe.

Pellet yeast   1 teaspoon
Raw honey   ½ teaspoon
Warm water   1¼ cups
Whole wheat flour   4½ cups
Egg yolk   1
Water   2 tablespoons
Sesame seeds, poppy seeds, or coarse salt   for coating

Dissolve yeast and honey in warm water; let mixture stand for 10 minutes. Gradually add flour until a soft dough forms, then knead on a floured surface for 7 to 8 minutes. Put dough in a buttered bowl, cover with a towel, and let rise in a warm place until doubled in bulk. Form dough into pretzels by making dough "snakes"—¼ inch thick and 8 inches long—twisting them into pretzel shape, and pressing dough together to fasten. Beat the egg yolk and water together; brush over pretzels. Roll the pretzels in seeds or sprinkle with salt. Place on an oiled cookie sheet and let rise in a warm place until doubled in bulk. Bake at 475° for 8 to 10 minutes, or until crisp and golden; watch the first batch carefully. Makes 3 dozen pretzels.

Carob Bread

This is one of my favorite breads; it's both versatile and delicious.

Pellet yeast 2 teaspoons
Blackstrap molasses 3 tablespoons
Warm water 1¾ cups
Sea salt ½ teaspoon
Noninstant powdered milk 3 tablespoons
Oil 2 tablespoons
Carob powder 3 tablespoons
Cloves ½ teaspoon
Vanilla 2 teaspoons
Currants ½ cup (optional)
Whole wheat flour 4 to 5 cups
Water for brushing

Dissolve yeast and molasses in warm water; set aside to bubble for 15 minutes. Add the next 7 ingredients plus 2 cups of flour; beat for 3 minutes, or until smooth. Add enough of the remaining flour so that dough comes away from the sides of the bowl. Turn out onto a floured surface and knead until smooth and elastic. Shape into a loaf, place in an oiled, standard 8-inch loaf pan, and cover with a towel. In a warm place, let dough rise until doubled in bulk, then bake at 325° for 50 to 60 minutes, brushing with water twice during the last 20 minutes to prevent bread from being overdone on top. Cool to allow easier slicing and fuller taste.
Note: This bread is perfect with meals, with dessert, as toast for breakfast, and especially as holiday gift bread. You may serve it with a hearty soup, with cheese and fruit, with ice cream, or with mint jelly.

Cinnamon-Raisin Bread

Pellet yeast   2 teaspoons
Raw honey   2 tablespoons
Warm water   ½ cup
Oil   ¼ cup
Cinnamon   1 teaspoon
Wheat germ   2 tablespoons
Unbleached flour   1 cup
Raisins   1 cup
Sea salt   ½ teaspoon
Whole wheat flour   1½ cups

Dissolve the yeast in honey and warm water; let rest 10 minutes. Add oil, cinnamon, wheat germ, and unbleached flour; stir well, then mix in raisins and salt. Gradually add whole wheat flour until dough becomes stiff, then turn out onto a floured surface and knead until smooth and elastic. Shape dough into loaf and place in an oiled, standard 8-inch loaf pan. Let rise, covered, in a warm place until doubled in bulk, then bake at 375° for 45 minutes. Remove from pan and cool loaf on its side on a wire rack.

Note: This bread makes very tasty breakfast toast.

Oatmeal-Currant Bread

Rolled oats   1½ cups
Boiling water   2 cups
Butter   ¼ cup
Milk   1 cup
Raw honey   ½ cup
Sea salt   1 tablespoon
Egg   1, beaten
Pellet yeast   1 tablespoon
Currants   ½ cup
Whole wheat flour   5 cups, plus as needed

Add oats to boiling water and cook 5 minutes. Remove from heat and add butter. When butter has melted, turn mixture into a large bowl and add milk, honey, and salt. Cool mixture to lukewarm, add egg and yeast, then allow mixture to stand 10 minutes, or until foaming occurs. Add currants, then gradually add flour, 1 cup at a time, stirring well after each addition. When the dough forms a ball, turn it onto a floured surface and knead until smooth and elastic; add more flour as needed to keep dough from being sticky. Shape dough into 2 loaves and place in oiled, standard 8-inch loaf pans. Let dough rise, covered, in a warm place until doubled in bulk, then bake at 350° for 40 minutes, or until bread sounds hollow when tapped. Cool loaves on their sides on a wire rack, then wrap and store overnight before slicing.

Note: This makes excellent toast.

Cranberry Bread

This bread is excellent with Thanksgiving dinner; it also makes good holiday gifts.

Pellet yeast   1 tablespoon
Raw honey   ¾ cup
Warm water   3 cups
Noninstant powdered milk   3 tablespoons
Oil   2 tablespoons
Sea salt   1 teaspoon
Whole wheat flour   8 to 9 cups
Fresh cranberries   2 cups chopped
Walnuts or pecans   ¾ cup chopped
Vanilla   2 teaspoons
Nutmeg   a dash

Dissolve yeast in honey and warm water; let mixture bubble for 10 minutes. Stir in powdered milk, oil, salt, and 4 cups of flour; stir very well for 5 minutes, then add cranberries, nuts, vanilla, and nutmeg. Gradually add the remaining flour until a stiff dough forms. Turn out onto a floured surface and knead until smooth and elastic. Shape dough into 8 small loaves or 2 large loaves and place in oiled 4-inch or standard 8-inch loaf pans. Cover with a towel and let rise in a warm place until doubled in bulk. Bake at 350°, 30 to 35 minutes for small loaves, 45 to 50 minutes for large loaves. Cool loaves on their sides on a wire rack. Makes 8 small loaves or 2 large loaves.

Variation: An egg glaze made of 1 egg beaten with a scant ¼ cup water may be brushed on the bread before baking to add to the special nature of a gift. Wrap in foil and decorate with ribbon and a card for the lucky recipient.

Pumpkin Bread

This is a great way to use the Great Pumpkin when Halloween has breathed its dying breath. Get the kids to help so you won't feel like a villain come November.

Pellet yeast   1 tablespoon
Blackstrap molasses or raw honey   2 tablespoons
Milk   1 cup, warm
Egg   1
Sea salt   ½ teaspoon
Pumpkin puree   ½ cup
Oil   2 tablespoons
Noninstant powdered milk   3 tablespoons
Bran   1 tablespoon
Cinnamon   ½ teaspoon
Ginger   ¼ teaspoon
Nutmeg   a dash
Whole wheat flour   3 to 4 cups
Milk or cream   for glazing
Apple butter or raw honey   for spreading (optional)

Dissolve yeast and molasses in warm milk; set aside 10 minutes. Add the next 9 ingredients, then mix in 2 cups of flour and stir well. Gradually add the remaining flour until dough becomes stiff. Turn out onto a floured surface and knead 5 to 7 minutes, or until smooth and elastic. Shape into loaf, place in an oiled, standard 8-inch loaf pan, and cover with a towel. Let rise in a warm place until doubled in bulk. Brush with milk, then bake at 350° for 50 to 60 minutes. Cool loaf on its side on a wire rack. Serve warm with apple butter.
Variation: This looks extra festive with a few sesame seeds sprinkled over the glaze.

Sweet Bread

This dough is a perfect base for cinnamon rolls, twists, filled breads, or other imaginative goodies. Use your favorite fillings and shapes.

Pellet yeast 2½ teaspoons
Warm water ⅔ cup
Milk ½ cup, scalded and cooled
Eggs 5
Lemon peel 2 teaspoons grated
Oil 2 tablespoons
Raw honey 1½ cups
Sea salt ½ teaspoon
Whole wheat flour 8 cups
Filling* up to 2 cups (optional)
Egg 1, beaten (optional)

Dissolve yeast in warm water and let stand 5 minutes. Add the next 6 ingredients plus 4 cups of flour; stir well. Slowly add the remaining flour, a little at a time, until a stiff dough forms. Turn out onto a floured surface and knead 10 minutes, or until the dough is smooth, elastic, and no longer sticky. Add the filling, shape dough into 2 loaves as you prefer, and place in 2 oiled, standard 8-inch loaf pans or on cookie sheet. Let rise, covered, in a warm place until doubled in bulk, then brush with egg for a shiny glaze and bake at 325° for 50 to 60 minutes. Cool before serving.
* Tasty, crunchy filling ingredients would be dates, almonds, walnuts, granola, cashews, figs, sesame seeds, currants, apricots, sliced apples or pears, or sunflower seeds. Or perhaps you could simply bury one lone almond in the loaf for a lucky guest to find! Use 3 tablespoons honey as a binder to your filling combination, and perhaps a dash of cinnamon or nutmeg. Dab in up to 2 tablespoons butter for extra richness. For a softer filling try Applesauce Filling (see Index), using only 1 recipe of it per loaf. You can fill the bread in different ways. Coarsely knead a crunchy filling into the dough or roll the dough out to a ¼-inch thickness, sprinkle it with filling, and roll it up. After filling, always allow the dough to rise—in a jelly roll pan or standard 8-inch loaf pan—until double in bulk, then bake as directed. If you make rolls, pastries, or twists from this dough, please reduce the baking time, for best results, to 20 to 30 minutes.

Whole Wheat English Muffins

Milk   1 cup
Raw honey   2 tablespoons
Sea salt   ½ teaspoon
Oil   ¼ cup
Pellet yeast   2 teaspoons
Apple juice or water   1 cup, warm
Whole wheat flour   8 cups
Coarse cornmeal   for sprinkling

Scald milk, then mix with honey, salt, and oil; set aside to cool. In another bowl, dissolve yeast in warm juice; set aside 10 minutes. Add cooled milk mixture and 3 cups of flour to yeast mixture; beat 5 minutes, or until very smooth. Add enough remaining flour, 1 cup at a time, to form a soft dough. Turn out onto a floured surface and knead until smooth and elastic. Place dough in an oiled bowl, cover with a towel, and let rise in a warm place until doubled in bulk. Punch dough down and divide into 2 balls. On a cornmeal-sprinkled surface, roll out each ball of dough to ½-inch thickness. Cut into 3-inch rounds and let muffins rise, covered, in a warm place until doubled in bulk. Carefully place muffins, cornmeal sides down, on a lightly oiled, medium hot griddle. Bake 15 minutes, or until lightly browned, then turn over and bake about 15 minutes more. Cool before serving. Makes 18 muffins.
Note: The muffins may be eaten right away, cooled and stored for several days, or cooled and frozen. In any case, they are smashing!

Sourdough English Muffins

Noninstant powdered milk   1 cup
Very warm water   1 cup
Sourdough Starter (see Index)   1 cup
Whole wheat flour   2¾ cups
Sea salt   1 teaspoon
Baking soda   ½ teaspoon
Fine cornmeal   for sprinkling

Mix together powdered milk, very warm water, Sourdough Starter, and 2 cups of flour; stir very well, cover loosely, and set aside in a warm place for at least 8 hours. Add remaining ¾ cup of flour, plus salt and baking soda; mix until dough is easy to handle. Turn out onto a floured surface and knead several minutes, then roll dough out on a cornmeal-sprinkled surface until dough is ½ inch thick. Cut into 3-inch rounds, then let muffins rise in a warm place until doubled in bulk. Bake, cornmeal sides down, on an oiled, medium hot griddle, for 10 minutes, or until golden brown, then turn and bake until browned. Cool before serving. Makes 12 muffins.

Note: The muffins may be cooled and served, stored for later use, or frozen.

Millet Rolls

Pellet yeast   1 teaspoon
Raw honey   1 tablespoon
Milk   1⅓ cups, warm
Oil   1 tablespoon
Sea salt   1 teaspoon
Kelp powder   ½ teaspoon
Millet flour   1 cup
Potato flour   ¼ cup
Whole wheat flour   3 cups
Raw honey   3 tablespoons
Water   3 tablespoons

Dissolve yeast and honey in warm milk, then add the next 5 ingredients plus 1½ cups of whole wheat flour. Stir mixture very rapidly for 5 minutes, then add enough of the remaining whole wheat flour to form a stiff dough. Turn out onto a floured surface and knead 5 minutes, or until smooth and elastic. Place dough in an oiled bowl, cover with a towel, and let rise in a warm place until doubled in bulk, then punch down and shape into your choice of roll shapes. Combine honey and water; brush over rolls. Place rolls in an oiled pan and let rise in a warm place until doubled in bulk. Bake at 375° for 20 minutes, or until done. Makes 12 rolls. Serve hot with butter and honey.

German Potato Rolls

Pellet yeast 2 teaspoons
Raw honey 1 tablespoon
Warm water 1½ cups
Potato flour ¾ cup
Oil 1 tablespoon
Noninstant powdered milk ¼ cup
Whole wheat flour 4 cups
Sea salt 1½ teaspoons

Dissolve yeast and honey in warm water; set aside 10 minutes. Add potato flour, oil, powdered milk, and 2 cups of whole wheat flour; mix well, then slowly add remaining flour and salt. Turn out onto a floured surface and knead 8 minutes, or until smooth and elastic. Shape dough into roll shape of your choice* and let rise, covered, in a warm place until doubled in bulk. Place in oiled muffin tins. Bake at 375° for about 20 minutes, depending on the size of the rolls; you may want to watch them carefully after 15 minutes to determine the proper amount of time. Makes 12 to 16 rolls. Serve immediately or cool and freeze.
* Try any of the following: triangles rolled up into crescent rolls; 3 or 4 little balls placed together in a muffin tin to make cloverleaf rolls; several layers of butter between pieces of dough in a muffin tin to make butterflake rolls; traditional egg shapes; traditional round shapes.
Variation: Brush rolls with egg white and decorate with sesame seeds or poppy seeds—very classy!

Sweet Rolls

This special recipe is from my grandma's neighbor, who cooks traditional, kosher foods. This is one of her favorite recipes.

Pellet yeast   1 tablespoon
Warm water   1⅔ cups
Oil   ½ cup
Raw honey   ¼ cup
Eggs   2
Sea salt   2 dashes
Whole wheat flour   5½ to 6½ cups
Anise seeds   2½ tablespoons
Egg   1
Water   scant ¼ cup
Sesame seeds   to taste
Raw sugar   to taste
Cinnamon   to taste
Butter   to taste

Dissolve yeast in ⅓ cup warm water; set aside 10 minutes. Add remaining warm water, plus oil, honey, eggs, salt, and 5 cups of flour. Stir well until dough becomes stiff, then turn out onto a floured surface and knead until smooth, elastic, and no longer sticky. Place dough in buttered bowl, cover with a towel, and let rise in a warm place until doubled in bulk. Punch dough down and divide in ½. Add anise seeds to ½ the dough, shape it into strips, and tie a small knot in each. Beat egg and water together, brush over rolls, and sprinkle with sesame seeds. Make cinnamon rolls with the remaining ½ of the dough by rolling it flat to ½-inch thickness and sprinkling it with sugar, cinnamon, and butter pats. Roll up dough and slice into rolls. Arrange both sets of rolls in buttered and sugared pans, put in a warm place, and allow to rise until doubled in bulk. Bake at 350° for 20 to 25 minutes. Cool before serving. Makes 2 dozen.

Variations: Knead in ⅔ cup chopped raisins, whole currants, or dates before shaping dough into rolls. Use this dough for cinnamon rolls, rolling out to ½-inch thickness and sprinkling with cinnamon, dabs of butter (up to 4 tablespoons), and 1 cup chopped walnuts. For cinnamon rolls with honey, add ½ cup raw honey and roll up (do not slice into individual rolls as the honey will burn at a very low temperature). Let rise in the pan until double in bulk, then bake up to 30 minutes. Cool, frost with a honey glaze, then slice and serve. For cinnamon rolls with raw sugar, add ½ cup raw sugar to the rolled-out dough. Roll up, slice at 1-inch intervals, and place in a baking pan into which ¼ cup raw sugar has been sprinkled. Let rolls rise until double in bulk, then bake for 25 minutes.

Kolacky

Pellet yeast 2 teaspoons
Milk 1 cup, warm
Butter ⅔ cup
Raw honey ⅓ cup
Sea salt ¼ teaspoon
Egg yolks 4
Whole wheat flour 4 to 4½ cups
Applesauce Filling (see Index) 1 cup

Sprinkle yeast into warm milk and dissolve. Add butter and stir until it is completely melted. Add honey, salt, and egg yolks, then slowly stir in flour until a soft dough forms which pulls away from the sides of the bowl. On a floured surface, and *without kneading*, shape the dough into small round roll shapes, about 2 inches in diameter. Press some filling into the center of each roll. You may either press in so that the filling will be visible once baked, adding extra drama to the appearance of the roll, or you may pinch the dough over the top of the filling, hiding the special treat inside. Then set rolls on oiled cookie sheets, cover with a cloth, and let rise in a warm place until doubled in bulk. Bake at 350° for 15 to 25 minutes, depending on the size of the rolls. Cool before serving. Makes about 12 to 14 rolls.
Variation: Roll the dough out to ½-inch thickness, fill, roll back up, and let rise in an oiled, standard 8-inch pan until doubled in bulk. Bake at 350° for 40 minutes. Makes a tasty bread.

Basic Bagels

Bagels seem to be catching on fairly rapidly these days as an interesting alternative to toast or sandwich bread. Since they're hard to find, except in a deli, some people think there is a great mystery to making them. The method is different, but not hard, and it produces delicious, chewy rolls for every occasion. Try them with cream cheese and smoked salmon, toast them and spread with butter and jam, or make up your own sandwich. However you try them, they will amaze your tastebuds and make you an instant bagel fan.

Pellet yeast   2 teaspoons
Raw honey   3 tablespoons
Warm water   1½ cups
Sea salt   1½ teaspoons
Whole wheat flour   4½ cups
Water   1 gallon

In a warm bowl* dissolve yeast and honey in warm water; let stand 10 minutes. Stir in salt and 1½ cups flour, then stir in enough of remaining flour to form a soft dough. Turn onto a floured surface and knead 10 minutes, adding more flour as needed, until dough is smooth and elastic. Cover dough and let stand 15 minutes, then punch it down. Take a small handful of dough and shape it into a ball. Flatten it into a pattie shape, then poke your finger through the middle and stretch it into a donut shape, about 4 to 5 inches in diameter. Repeat with remaining dough. Cover bagels with a towel and let rise in a warm place until almost double. Bring water to a boil, then carefully drop in a few bagels at a time, maintaining the boil. Simmer bagels for 7 minutes per side, then remove (a chopstick works well) and cool on a wire rack. Place bagels on an unoiled cookie sheet and bake at 375° for 30 to 35 minutes. Cool and serve, or wrap and store for later use. Makes 12 bagels.
* Pour warm water into your bowl, let it sit until bowl is warm, then discard water. This is a good idea for making any yeast bread great.
Variations: Use rye flour, molasses, and caraway seeds for a new taste. You can also add sautéed minced onion, grated Cheddar cheese, or herbs. All are delicious.

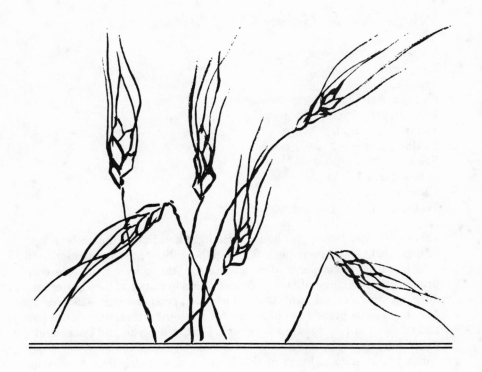

Quick Breads, Muffins, and Biscuits

Whole Wheat–Honey Quick Bread

Butter   2 tablespoons
Raw honey   1 cup
Egg   1
Orange peel   1½ tablespoons grated
Lemon peel   1 teaspoon grated
Whole wheat flour   2 cups
Baking powder   2½ teaspoons
Sea salt   ½ teaspoon
Wheat germ   ¼ cup
Orange juice   ¾ cup
Walnuts   1 cup chopped

Cream together butter and honey until light and fluffy, then mix in egg, orange peel, and lemon peel. Sift together flour, baking powder, and salt; blend in wheat germ; then alternately add to butter mixture with orange juice, mixing only until blended. Fold in nuts and turn batter into an oiled and floured, standard 8-inch loaf pan. Bake at 325° for 70 minutes. Allow bread to cool in pan for 5 minutes, then turn out of pan and cool loaf on its side on a wire rack. Wrap the bread and let it stand 1 to 2 days before slicing.

Note: The orangy richness of this bread makes it delicious as toast or stuffing, and delicious with garden sandwich fillings.

Bran Bread or Muffins

Two slices of bran bread or two bran muffins will provide most adults' daily roughage requirement.

Bran   3 cups
Unbleached flour   1 cup
Whole wheat flour   1 cup
Wheat germ   ½ cup
Noninstant powdered milk or buttermilk   3 heaping tablespoons
Baking soda   2 teaspoons
Baking powder   2 rounded teaspoons
Sea salt   ½ teaspoon
Orange juice or water   3 cups, warm
Eggs   2
Raw honey   ½ cup
Dates or figs   1 cup chopped or
    Currants   1 cup

Mix together the first 8 ingredients; add remaining ingredients and mix well. Pour into 2 greased and floured, standard 8-inch loaf pans or fill 24 greased and floured muffin tins ⅔ full. Bake 350°, 35 to 40 minutes for bread, 30 minutes for muffins. Serve hot; cool remaining loaves or muffins and freeze or store airtight.

Incredible Cornbread

Trial and error finally resulted in the invention of this light and delicious cornbread. The kids really love it.

Orange juice ½ cup
Plain yogurt ½ cup
Noninstant powdered milk 2 tablespoons
Eggs 2
Soy oil ¼ cup
Whole wheat pastry flour 1 cup
Blackstrap molasses 1 tablespoon
Sea salt ½ teaspoon
Baking powder 1 tablespoon
Fine cornmeal 1 cup
Raw honey or apple butter for spreading (optional)

Thoroughly mix the first 10 ingredients, then pour into an oiled and floured 8 by 8-inch baking pan. Bake at 350° for 30 minutes, or until done. Serve hot with honey.
Note: Serve this cornbread with clam chowder for a hearty family (or company) meal. Couple with hot apple cider, sliced fruit, and cheese for an elegant autumn repast.

Super Breakfast Bread

Buttermilk or plain yogurt 2 cups
Raw honey ½ cup
Blackstrap molasses ¼ cup
Baking soda 2 teaspoons
Sea salt ½ teaspoon
Whole wheat flour 1½ cups
Unbleached flour 1 cup
Wheat germ ½ cup
Currants ½ cup or
    Dried fruit ½ cup chopped

Preheat oven to 400°. Mix together the first 5 ingredients; stir well. Add whole wheat flour, unbleached flour, and wheat germ, then stir in currants. Pour batter into an oiled and floured, standard 8-inch loaf pan. Lower oven to 350°, put pan in oven, and bake 1 hour. Cool loaf on its side on a wire rack; store overnight before serving.
Note: This is best as toast and is terrific with orange marmalade.

Swedish Flatbread

Crisp, delicious, and low in calories.

Whole wheat or graham flour 1 cup
Rye flour 1 cup
Rolled oats ½ cup
Sesame seeds ¼ cup
Walnuts ½ cup finely chopped
Raisins or currants ⅓ cup
Buttermilk or plain yogurt 1 cup
Sea salt ¼ teaspoon
Baking soda ½ teaspoon
Cheese or spreads (optional)

Combine the first 9 ingredients, mix very well, and roll out on a floured surface. Place dough on a 13-inch cookie sheet and roll out as far as it will go on the cookie sheet. Bake at 400° for 10 minutes, then turn and continue baking until evenly done on both sides. Cool on a wire rack, then serve with cheese.

Variations: You can play with this recipe very easily. Make herbed or seasoned rye crisp with the addition of 2 to 3 teaspoons of 1 or more herbs, sautéed minced onion, chopped parsley, or caraway seeds; seasoning salt can be sprinkled over the dough.

Best Carrot Bread

My sweet next-door neighbor has shared several of her recipes with me. This one is especially good.

Eggs 3
Raw sugar 2 cups
Oil 1½ cups
Carrots 2 cups grated
Crushed pineapple 1 cup, partially drained
Pecans or walnuts 1 cup chopped
Vanilla 1 tablespoon
Whole wheat pastry flour 3 cups
Sea salt ½ teaspoon
Baking soda 1 teaspoon
Cinnamon 2 teaspoons

Completely blend eggs, sugar, and oil; you may use a blender. Place in a bowl along with carrots, pineapple, nuts, and vanilla. Stir in remaining ingredients, blend well, and pour into an oiled and floured, standard 8-inch loaf pan. Bake at 325° for 1 hour. Cool in the pan for several minutes before cooling on a wire rack.

Variation: This makes luscious cupcakes. Fill greased or paper-lined tins ⅔ full, then bake at 325° for 25 to 30 minutes. Cool, then frost with my Honey–Cream Cheese Frosting (see Index). With this treat, big smiles will be your reward.

Gluten-Free Millet-Carrot Bread

Millet flour   1 cup
Boiling water   ¾ cup
Soy flour   ½ cup
Baking powder   1 teaspoon
Egg yolks   3
Oil   3 tablespoons
Raw honey   1 teaspoon
Kelp powder   a dash
Carrots   1 cup grated
Egg whites   3, beaten until stiff

Mix together millet flour and boiling water; set aside to cool. Thoroughly beat together the next 7 ingredients, then add the cooled millet mixture. Fold in the egg whites, pour batter into an oiled and floured, standard 8-inch loaf pan, and bake at 375° for 40 minutes. Serve immediately for best flavor.
Note: Because of the egg whites, it is necessary to get this into the oven as quickly as possible for maximum success. This bread is delicious with cream cheese for a breakfast or teatime treat.

Banana Nut Bread

Butter   ½ cup
Raw honey   1 cup
Eggs   2
Ripe bananas   1 cup mashed
Lemon juice   1 teaspoon
Whole wheat pastry flour   2 cups
Baking soda   1 tablespoon
Sea salt   ½ teaspoon
Walnuts*   1 cup chopped

Cream butter, then drizzle in honey and beat until light and fluffy. Add next 6 ingredients, stir well, then fold in nuts, mixing quickly. Pour batter into a greased, standard 8-inch loaf pan and bake at 375° for 75 minutes. Cool loaf on its side on a wire rack; for improved flavor, let stand overnight, if you can stand the temptation.

* Pecans, almonds, or sunflower seeds could be substituted.

Note: When creaming honey into a recipe, a slow and steady stream of honey, beaten in steadily, will increase the overall volume of your batter and the lightness of your final product. Resist the temptation to dump the honey in and stir—slow and steady makes for light and fluffy.

Mom's Date Nut Bread

Dates 1 cup chopped
Boiling water 1 cup
Butter 1 tablespoon
Whole wheat pastry flour 2 cups
Baking powder 1 tablespoon
Sea salt ½ teaspoon
Raw honey ¾ cup
Egg 1
Walnuts* 1 cup chopped

Combine the dates, boiling water, and butter; set aside until cool. Combine the remaining ingredients, add the cooled date mixture, and mix well. Pour into an oiled, standard 8-inch loaf pan, let stand 20 minutes, then bake at 325° for 50 to 60 minutes, or until done. Cool on a wire rack. You may eat this immediately, but the flavor improves after 24 hours, so wrap after cooling. This also freezes well.

* Sunflower seeds, pecans, or almonds can be substituted.

Zucchini Bread

I know every book has a recipe for zucchini bread, but this is the best one I've ever tried. The subtle spices and the rich zucchini taste make this a real treat. There's always one loaf gone before they even cool.

Oil   1 cup
Eggs   3
Raw honey or raw brown sugar*   2 cups
Zucchini   2 cups grated
Vanilla   1 tablespoon
Sea salt   1 teaspoon
Baking soda   1 teaspoon
Allspice   1 teaspoon
Cinnamon   1 teaspoon
Cloves   1 teaspoon
Baking powder   ½ teaspoon
Whole wheat pastry flour   3 cups
Walnuts   1 cup chopped

In blender, mix together oil, eggs, and honey. Mix together the next 9 ingredients, add honey mixture, and mix well. Fold in nuts, then pour into 2 oiled and floured, standard 8-inch loaf pans. Bake at 325° for 1 hour. Cool on wire racks before serving. Makes excellent gifts and stores well in freezer up to 6 months.
* Use 1 cup each for even richer flavor.

Millet Muffins

Eggs 4
Soy or sunflower oil ½ cup
Lecithin granules or liquid lecithin 2 teaspoons
Raw honey ¾ cup
Vanilla or powdered vanilla ¼ teaspoon
Millet flour 1 cup
Soy flour ¼ cup
Whole wheat pastry flour 1 cup
Rice polishings* ¼ cup
Baking powder 2 teaspoons
Sea salt ½ teaspoon
Milk ¾ cup
Raisins or currants 1 cup or
      Dates or figs 1 cup chopped

In a blender, mix together the first 5 ingredients. In a bowl, mix together the next 6 ingredients. Add the egg mixture and the milk, stir well, and add raisins. Fill oiled muffin tins ⅔ full and bake at 350° for 25 minutes. Serve hot for best flavor. Makes 12 muffins.
* Rice polishings are also known as rice bran. If you can't find either one, brown rice flour or wheat bran will do.
Note: Good with breakfast; also good at dinner with a creamy vegetable soup.

Those Famous Health Bran Muffins

Two per day equal the minimum adult requirement for roughage.

Bran   3 cups
Boiling water   ¾ cup
Butter   ½ cup
Raw honey   ¾ cup
Eggs   2
Buttermilk   2 cups
Whole wheat flour   1¾ cups
Wheat germ   ¾ cup
Baking soda   2½ teaspoons
Sea salt   ½ teaspoon
Dates or walnuts   1 cup chopped (optional)

Mix together the bran, boiling water, and butter; set aside. Mix together the next 7 ingredients, add dates, then add the bran mixture; stir well. Fill oiled or paper-lined muffin tins ¾ full and bake at 400° for 20 minutes. Cool before serving. Makes 12 muffins.
Note: These will keep for up to 6 weeks in the refrigerator. They may also be frozen.

Molasses Bran Muffins

Bran   1 cup
Milk   ¾ cup, warm
Whole wheat pastry flour   1 cup
Baking powder   2 teaspoons
Baking soda   ½ teaspoon
Sea salt   ¼ teaspoon
Blackstrap molasses   ½ cup
Eggs   2
Oil   2 tablespoons
Raisins   ½ cup

Soak bran in warm milk; set aside several minutes, then add the remaining ingredients and stir until well mixed. Fill oiled muffin tins ⅔ full and bake at 400° for 20 minutes. Makes 12 muffins.
Note: This recipe can be baked in a microwave oven; check your model for specific time and setting. These are quite good for breakfast with raw honey.

Blueberry Muffins or Bread

Raw honey ½ cup
Butter 6 tablespoons
Eggs 2
Milk ¾ cup
Whole wheat flour 2½ cups
Baking powder 1 tablespoon
Sea salt ½ teaspoon
Vanilla 1 teaspoon
Fresh blueberries 1½ cups
Walnuts ¾ cup chopped

Cream together the honey and butter, then add the next 6 ingredients; blend just long enough for everything to get wet. Fold in blueberries and nuts, then fill greased muffin tins ⅔ full or pour into a greased, standard 8-inch loaf pan. Bake at 350°, 25 minutes for muffins, 75 minutes for bread. Makes 12 to 16 muffins.

Honey Biscuits

Butter 1 cup
Raw honey 1 cup
Eggs 2
Whole wheat pastry flour 4 cups
Baking powder 1 teaspoon
Sea salt ½ teaspoon
Pumpkin pie spice 2 teaspoons

Melt the butter in a saucepan, add honey, and boil 2 minutes over low heat, stirring occasionally. Remove from heat and cool, then add eggs. Sift together the remaining ingredients, then combine with honey mixture and mix well. Set dough aside for 10 minutes, then shape into 1½-inch balls, press onto an ungreased cookie sheet, and flatten with your hand or with a fork. Bake at 350° for 15 minutes and serve hot for breakfast, lunch, dinner, or with tea. Makes 24 biscuits.
Note: Honey Butter (see Index), preserves, or maple syrup are all terrific with these delicate and tasty biscuits.

Whole Wheat Mix for Biscuits or Pancakes

Many of our friends have taken this mix camping, and they say it is versatile, tasty, and handy. It's also good in the kitchen.

Whole wheat pastry flour   8 cups
Baking powder   ¼ cup plus 2 teaspoons
Sea salt   2 teaspoons
Noninstant powdered milk   2 cups
Raw sugar or honey   ½ cup
Powdered vanilla or cinnamon   to taste (optional)
Oil   1½ cups

Stir together all ingredients until crumbly. Store in an airtight container until needed. Use within 3 months. Makes about 11 cups of mix. To make Whole Wheat Biscuits, add ⅓ cup water per cup of mix. Shape into biscuits and bake on a greased cookie sheet 12 to 15 minutes at 350°. To make Whole Wheat Pancakes, add 1 cup water or apple juice and 1 egg per cup of mix. Fry on a hot, greased griddle until golden brown on both sides.

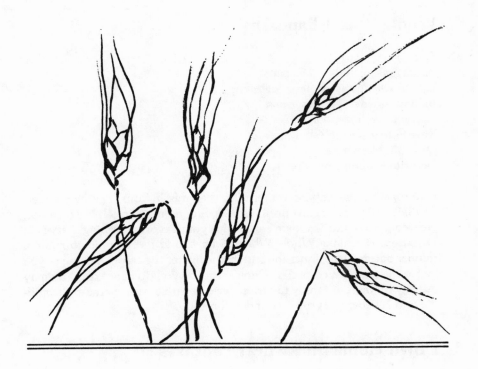

Pancakes,
Waffles, and
Doughnuts

Whole Wheat Pancakes

Egg 1
Buttermilk or milk 1½ cups
Whole wheat pastry flour 1½ cups
Baking powder 2 teaspoons
Sea salt ¼ teaspoon
Raw honey 2 tablespoons
Oil 2 tablespoons
Favorite toppings or spreads

Beat together the egg and buttermilk, then mix in flour, baking powder, and salt. Add honey, mix until just blended, then stir in oil. Fry on a hot, greased griddle until golden; serve with your favorite topping. Serves 2.
Variation: To make Whole Wheat Crepes, add more liquid to make a thinner batter (the thinner the batter, the lighter the crepe), testing as you go for the texture you prefer. Cook crepes as you do pancakes. You may use any filling; our family favorite is crepes with cream cheese in the middle and Blueberry Syrup (see Index) on top.

Down Home Buckwheat Pancakes

Egg 1, well beaten
Milk 1 cup
Blackstrap molasses 2 tablespoons
Oil 2 tablespoons
Stone-ground buckwheat flour 1 cup
Baking powder 1 teaspoon
Sea salt ¼ teaspoon
Maple syrup, raw honey, or applesauce for topping

Mix together the first 7 ingredients just until wet. Fry on an oiled griddle until golden, turning once. Serve with maple syrup. Serves 2.
Note: The darkness of most items made with buckwheat comes from the molasses rather than the buckwheat. If you would prefer a more delicate flavor and color, substitute honey for molasses in equal amounts.

Cornmeal Mountain Pancakes

Egg   1
Buttermilk   1½ cups
Whole wheat pastry flour   1 cup
Sea salt   ½ teaspoon
Baking soda   ½ teaspoon
Baking powder   2 teaspoons
Fine or coarse cornmeal   ¼ cup

Mix together all ingredients until wet, then fry on a hot, greased griddle until golden brown, turning once. Serves 2.
Note: Maple syrup is especially good with these pancakes.

Pineapple Pancakes

Wheat germ   1 cup
Whole wheat pastry flour   3 cups
Baking powder   2 tablespoons
Sea salt   ½ teaspoon
Blackstrap molasses   3 tablespoons
Crushed pineapple in juice   1 cup, drained
Pineapple juice or milk   3 to 4 cups
Oil   ⅓ cup
Maple syrup, honey, jam, or yogurt   for topping

Combine the first 5 ingredients, then add pineapple and 2 cups of juice. Stir until ingredients thicken, then gradually add the remaining juice until batter is as thick as you prefer (the thicker the batter, the thicker the pancake). Stir in oil and mix well. Fry on a hot, greased griddle until golden, turning once. Serve with maple syrup. Serves 4 to 6.

Best Blintzes

This is an excellent breakfast for the self-indulgent, dessert for most anyone else.

Whole wheat pastry flour 1 cup
Baking powder 1 tablespoon
Raw honey 2 tablespoons
Sea salt ¼ teaspoon
Eggs 2
Milk 1½ cups
Oil 3 tablespoons
Filling
Sour cream topping
Blueberries topping

Stir together the first 7 ingredients; cover and set aside 1 hour. Pour 2 tablespoons of batter into a hot, oiled 6-inch skillet; tilt the pan to spread the batter around and cook about 1 minute, or until brown. Turn and cook just until the batter sets. Lay each blintze on a tea towel, brown side up. Spread the brown side of each blintze with 1 tablespoon of filling, roll each up envelope style, and fry each in butter over medium heat until golden brown. Serve with sour cream and blueberries for a classic treat. Makes 12 blintzes.

Filling

Cottage cheese 1 cup
Raw honey 1 tablespoon
Cinnamon or nutmeg a dash
Egg 1, beaten

Mix together all ingredients.

Buttermilk Waffles

Whole wheat pastry flour   1¾ cups
Baking powder   2 teaspoons
Baking soda   1 teaspoon
Sea salt   ¼ teaspoon
Buttermilk   1½ cups
Oil   5 tablespoons
Egg yolks   2
Egg whites   2, beaten until stiff
Butter and honey, peanut butter and sliced bananas, or favorite toppings

Combine the first 7 ingredients, mixing until all ingredients are wet. Fold in egg whites, then cook in greased waffle iron until golden. Serve with butter and honey. Serves 2 to 3.

Whole Wheat Doughnuts

These quick treats will intrigue the breakfast, coffee-break, or snack crowd.

Eggs   3
Raw sugar   1 cup
Blackstrap molasses   1 tablespoon
Milk, buttermilk, or plain yogurt   ¾ cup
Oil   3 tablespoons
Orange peel   2 teaspoons grated
Whole wheat pastry flour   4½ cups
Baking powder   2 tablespoons
Sea salt   1 teaspoon
Nutmeg   ½ teaspoon
Coconut or peanut oil   for deep frying
Carob-Flavored Frosting (see Index)   (optional)

Blend together the first 5 ingredients. Dash in orange peel, then gradually stir in the flour, baking powder, salt, and nutmeg. Stir very well, then divide dough in ½ and roll out each to ½-inch thickness. Cut with a doughnut cutter and deep fry at 375° for 1 minute per side, or until golden brown. Remove and drain; frost if desired. Makes 24 to 30 doughnuts.
Variation: Brush doughnut with raw honey and roll in chopped nuts, shredded or flaked coconut, or raw sugar.

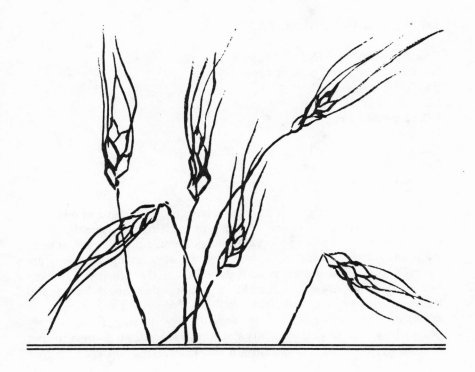

Granola
and
Hiker's Mix

Gail's Homemade Granola

Four flaked-grain cereal*   8 cups
Rolled oats   4 cups, plus as needed
Sunflower seeds   2 cups
Sesame seeds   1½ cups
Wheat germ   2 cups
Cinnamon   2 teaspoons
Soy oil   1 cup
Raw honey   ½ cup
Raw sugar   1 cup

Place flaked cereals and rolled oats in a large roasting pan and mix well. Bake uncovered at 375° for 10 minutes, stirring occasionally. Add sunflower seeds, stir, and bake 5 minutes more. Sprinkle with sesame seeds and bake another 5 minutes. Mix in wheat germ and toast mixture carefully, just until brown around the edges of the pan; remove from oven. Sprinkle with cinnamon and toss. Boil together the oil, honey, and sugar, stirring only occasionally until sugar dissolves and mixture is smooth; pour over cereal and mix well. If, after tossing, the cereal appears sticky, add more rolled oats and toss again. Allow granola to cool completely, then store in an airtight container. This will keep up to 4 weeks. Makes 6 pounds.

* Any cereal product that contains rolled oats, rolled wheat, rolled barley, and rolled rye.

Variations: You may tailor this granola to your family's taste with the addition of raisins, almonds, coconut, dates, walnuts, or any other nutritious ingredient you want. Add with the cereal during the toasting process if you want them toasted, or after the syrup is stirred in if you want them raw.

Super Health Granola

Rolled or flaked wheat, oats, rye, and barley   5 cups
Bran   1 cup
Sesame seeds   1½ cups
Wheat germ   1½ cups
Soy flour   1 cup, sifted
Noninstant powdered milk   1 cup
Cashew halves and pieces   1 cup
Sunflower seeds   1 cup
Raw honey   1 cup
Oil   1 cup
Dates   1 cup chopped
Raisins or currants   1 cup

In a large bowl, mix together the first 8 ingredients; toss well, making sure there are no lumps. Heat together the honey and oil over medium high heat until mixture boils, then pour it over the tossed mixture, blending well. Arrange granola in a large roasting pan and bake uncovered at 250° for 1 hour, or until lightly browned; stir every 10 to 12 minutes. Add dates and raisins immediately and cool thoroughly. Store in an airtight container. Keeps up to 4 weeks. Makes 16 cups.

David's Hiker's Mix

Our youngest son, David, loves the Hiker's Mix and wanted it named after him. Just for you, Tiger!

Almonds   ½ part
Walnuts   ½ part
Dates   1 part
Currants   1 part
Large flaked coconut   1 part
Sunflower seeds   1 part
Raw peanuts   1 part
Raw cashews   2 parts
Salted or unsalted soy nuts   2 parts, toasted

Mix all ingredients together and store in an airtight container. Serve anytime.

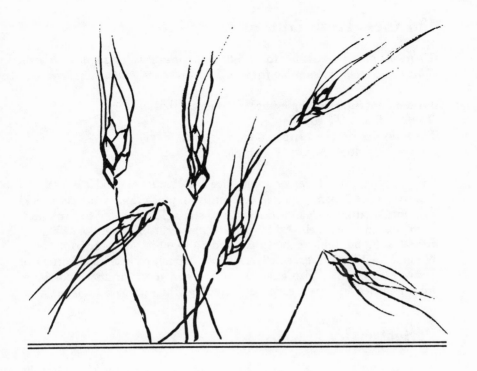

Desserts
and
Pastries

Sugarless Fresh Fruit or Berry Pie

Delicious pies are possible for us all, and without using sugar or honey. This basic recipe is suitable for any fruit or berry your heart desires.

Frozen concentrated apple juice   6 ounces, thawed
Tapioca flour   ¼ cup
Fresh berries or sliced fruit   4 cups
Pastry   for double-crust, 9-inch pie

In a saucepan, mix together apple juice and tapioca flour. Heat over low heat and cook, stirring almost constantly (tapioca flour sets very quickly), until mixture is clear. Add fruit and stir well. Simmer 1 to 2 minutes, then pour into pie shell. Add top crust, make slits in it, and bake at 375° for 40 to 50 minutes for berry pie and 50 to 60 minutes for fruit pie.
Note: This filling is especially tasty with fresh-picked blackberries or strawberries, and is also effective with a strawberry-rhubarb combination. Peaches and cherries are outstanding when prepared this way.

Perfect Flaky Piecrust

There are millions of pie-makers in my family, so all my life I carefully forgot to learn how to make pies, knowing that someone else would make them if I did something else. Alas, one day about a week after I was married, my husband said, "How about making a banana creme pie?" There was a long silence while I contemplated two answers: "What's the matter, do you have a broken arm?" and "I never learned how." I ended up trying both, and neither worked. The next time he went to the grocery store, a can of pumpkin appeared in the pantry and began staring at me together with a bunch of bananas standing guard on top of the refrigerator. I began to get nervous. At the same time, he let my mom know that the time for me to learn to make pies was upon us all. At Christmas, a pastry cutter appeared in my stocking. There was no backing out, so one Saturday morning, when it was quiet and everyone had left me alone, I made two pumpkin pies. To my surprise, they were really pretty good. A few weeks later, I got really brave and tried banana creme from scratch. They also turned out well. After we bought the Wheatex Mill, I began baking with better flours. One day I thought I would try making a piecrust with whole wheat pastry flour. I did all the right things, but after I chilled the dough and rolled it out, I had such a patch job as had never been done. (It even broke apart in the pan!) I thought I'd really blown it, but I kept patching anyway, made the pie, and baked it. Surprise! It was the flakiest crust I have ever tasted — flavorful and light. This piecrust is the result of much practice and recipe refinement.

Whole wheat pastry flour 1½ cups
Wheat germ ½ cup
Sea salt or kelp powder 1 teaspoon
Butter ⅔ cup
Ice water up to ¼ cup

Combine flour, wheat germ, and salt. Cut in butter with a pastry blender or 2 knives until mixture forms pea-sized crumbs. Chill mixture for several minutes, then sprinkle with ice water and pat together to form a ball. Wrap in waxed paper and chill 1 hour, then remove from refrigerator and set aside at room temperature for 15 minutes. Remove dough from waxed paper, divide in half, and roll out on a floured surface, handling as little as possible. Arrange dough in 9-inch pie tin and crimp edges firmly. Fill and bake as directed. For a baked pie shell, pierce the dough with a fork and bake at 425° for 10 minutes. Makes 1 double-crust pie or 2 pie shells.

Gluten-Free Barley Piecrust

Oil ¼ cup
Water 3½ tablespoons
Sea salt 1 teaspoon
Barley flour 1½ cups
Baking powder 1 teaspoon

Thoroughly mix oil, water, and salt. Add barley flour and baking powder, pack dough well together, and roll out to make crust. Place dough in 9-inch pan; fill and bake as directed. For a baked pie shell, pierce dough with a fork and bake at 400° for 15 minutes. Makes 1 pie shell. This is good for refrigerated or frozen pies.

Granola Piecrust

Butter 3 tablespoons
Raw honey 2 tablespoons
Super Granola (see Index) 2 to 2½ cups

Melt butter and honey together in small saucepan over low heat; stir in granola. Press warm mixture into 9-inch pie tin, bake at 325° for 10 minutes, then cool and fill. Makes 1 pie shell for any refrigerated or frozen pie.

Note: This pie shell is especially good with Gail's Cheesecake (see Index) or with strawberry filling as made in the Sugarless Fresh Fruit or Berry Pie recipe (see Index).

Gail's Cheesecake

Cream cheese or Neufchâtel cheese* 16 ounces at room temperature
Raw honey ¾ cup
Eggs 4
Vanilla 1 teaspoon
Lemon peel 1 tablespoon grated
Graham Cracker Crust
Sour cream 1 cup
Fresh fruit topping (optional) or
  Fresh Berry Syrup (see Index) topping (optional)

Cream together cream cheese and honey, adding honey slowly, until mixture is light and fluffy. Add eggs, 1 at a time, mixing each in thoroughly. Stir in vanilla and lemon peel, pour filling into Graham Cracker Crust, and bake at 300° for 1 hour. Cool cheesecake, then frost with sour cream. Top with fruit just before serving.

* Neufchâtel cheese tastes like cream cheese, but is lower in calories and less expensive.

Graham Cracker Crust*

Butter 3 tablespoons
Raw honey 2 tablespoons
Graham cracker squares 16, crumbled

Melt butter and honey together in an 8-inch pie tin, quiche pan, or 8 by 8-inch baking pan. Add crumbled crackers to pan, mix well, then press mixture to the sides and bottom of the pan, forming an even crust. Bake at 325° for 10 minutes, then cool.

* Granola Piecrust also is delicious with this cheesecake.

Delicious Apple Cake

The dear lady who lives next door to our old mill brought me this recipe, thinking I might like it. I surely do.

Golden Delicious apples   1½ cups grated
Raw honey   ½ cup
Water   ½ cup
Currants   ½ cup
Butter   ¼ cup
Cloves   ¼ teaspoon
Cinnamon   ½ teaspoon
Whole wheat pastry flour   1¾ cups
Baking powder   ½ teaspoon
Baking soda   ½ teaspoon
Sea salt   ½ teaspoon
Spice-Flavored Frosting (see Index)   (optional)

In a saucepan, combine the first 7 ingredients and simmer 5 minutes. Cool, then mix in flour, baking powder, baking soda, and salt. Spoon batter into an oiled and floured 8-inch square pan; bake at 375° for 35 minutes. Cool, frost, and serve.

Variation: Fill oiled and floured cupcake tins ⅔ full and bake at 375° for 20 minutes. Cool, frost, and serve for dessert, or spread with butter and honey and serve for breakfast. Makes 12 cupcakes.

Applesauce Cake

Oil   ⅔ cup
Raw honey   1½ cups
Large eggs   2
Thick, unsweetened applesauce   2½ cups
Whole wheat pastry flour   1½ cups
Unbleached flour   1½ cups
Baking powder   2 rounded teaspoons
Sea salt   1 teaspoon
Cinnamon   2 teaspoons
Cloves   1 teaspoon
Nutmeg   ¼ teaspoon
Dates   2 cups chopped or
    Raisins   2 cups
Vanilla   2 teaspoons
Nuts*   1 cup chopped (optional)

Blend together the oil, honey, and eggs, then stir in applesauce. Sift together the next 7 ingredients and add to applesauce mixture. Fold in dates, vanilla, and nuts; pour batter into an oiled and floured 13 by 9 by 2-inch cake pan. Bake at 350° for 35 minutes, or until done. Cool on wire rack before serving.
* Walnuts are best, but almonds and cashews are good if they are finely chopped.
Variation: Pour batter into 2 oiled and floured, standard 8-inch loaf pans and bake at 350° for 1 hour, or until done.

Lemon Loaf

Butter   ½ cup
Raw honey   ⅔ cup
Eggs   2
Lemon peel   of 1 lemon, grated
Vanilla   1 teaspoon
Lemon juice   1 tablespoon
Whole wheat pastry flour   1½ cups
Baking powder   1 teaspoon
Sea salt   a dash
Milk   ⅓ cup

Cream together butter and honey, drizzling in honey as butter is whipped to fluffiness. Add eggs, lemon peel, vanilla, and lemon juice; beat well. Mix together flour, baking powder, and salt; alternately add to honey mixture with milk, and beat until smooth. Spread batter into an oiled and floured, standard 8-inch loaf pan; bake at 350° for 45 minutes. Cool and serve.

Note: This cake is great with a lemon pudding topping, as a shortcake base, and with ice cream.

Grandma's Banana Cake

This is the cake my grandma makes whenever she's expecting a crowd. It's a good standby, and easy to make in a hurry.

Butter   ½ cup
Raw sugar   1½ cups
Eggs   2
Lemon juice   1 teaspoon
Bananas   ¾ cup mashed
Whole wheat pastry flour   2 cups
Baking powder   ½ teaspoon
Baking soda   ¾ teaspoon
Sea salt   ¼ teaspoon
Walnuts   ½ cup chopped
Lemon-Flavored Frosting (see Index)   (optional)

Cream together butter and sugar, then add eggs, lemon juice, and bananas; beat until fluffy. Add flour, baking powder, baking soda, and salt; mix well, then stir in nuts. Pour batter into an oiled and floured, 8-inch square or standard 8-inch loaf pan and bake at 350° for 30 minutes. Cool and frost.

Sour Cream–Orange Cake

This makes a light, delicate, and moist cake.

Raisins   1 cup
Large orange   1, peeled and in segments
Raw honey   ½ cup
Eggs   2
Sour cream   1 cup
Butter   ¼ cup
Whole wheat pastry flour   2½ cups
Baking soda   1 teaspoon

Put raisins, orange segments, honey, and eggs in blender and chop together. Add sour cream and butter; blend a few seconds more. Pour mixture into a bowl and add flour and baking soda; stir well. Pour batter into an oiled and floured, 8-inch square or standard 8-inch loaf pan and bake at 350° for 35 minutes.

Yogurt-Carrot Cake

Butter   1 cup
Raw sugar   1½ cups
Eggs   4
Lemon peel   1 teaspoon grated
Cinnamon   1 teaspoon
Vanilla   1 teaspoon
Plain yogurt   1 cup
Whole wheat pastry flour   2½ cups
Baking soda   1 teaspoon
Baking powder   1½ teaspoons
Sea salt   ¼ teaspoon
Carrots   2½ cups grated
Nuts*   ¾ cup chopped
My Honey–Cream Cheese Frosting (see Index)   (optional)

Cream together butter and sugar, then add next 5 ingredients; mix well. Blend in flour, baking soda, baking powder, and salt, then fold in carrots and nuts. Turn batter into an oiled and floured 10-inch bundt pan, 10-inch tube pan, or standard 8-inch loaf pan. Bake at 350° for 40 minutes, or until golden brown. Cool in pan, then turn out and cool on wire rack. Frost for a classic taste combination.

* Walnuts are best; almonds, cashews, and sunflower seeds are also good.

Carob Devil's Food Cake

Butter   ½ cup
Carob powder   ½ cup
Sour cream   1½ cups
Raw sugar   1½ cups
Blackstrap molasses   1 tablespoon
Eggs   3, beaten
Whole wheat pastry flour   2 cups
Baking soda   1 teaspoon
Sea salt   ¼ teaspoon
Vanilla   1 teaspoon
Instant decaffeinated coffee   1 teaspoon
Cloves   ½ teaspoon
Carob-Flavored Frosting or
    Basic Spreadable Frosting (see Index)   (optional)

Melt butter and carob powder together over low heat; set aside to cool. In a mixing bowl, combine the next 7 ingredients and beat 2 minutes, scraping the sides of the bowl frequently. Add the vanilla, coffee, and cloves, and beat another minute. Blend in carob mixture just until well mixed, and pour into 2 oiled and floured, round 8-inch cake pans. Bake at 350° for 35 minutes. Allow cake to cool in pans before removing to a wire rack, as the cake can be very fragile when warm. Frost and serve.

Gluten-Free Devil's Food Cake

Brown rice flour   1½ cups
Carob powder   ½ cup
Cloves   ½ teaspoon
Baking powder   1 teaspoon
Raw honey   ½ cup
Eggs   2
Butter   6 tablespoons
Milk   ½ cup
Plain yogurt   2 tablespoons
Carob-Flavored Frosting (see Index)   (optional) or
      Whipped cream   for topping (optional)

Mix together flour, carob powder, cloves, and baking powder. Whip
together honey, eggs, butter, and ¼ cup milk until fluffy. Add flour mixture, beat until smooth, then add remaining ¼ cup milk and continue
beating. Add yogurt and beat until batter is smooth again, then pour into
an oiled and floured, round 8-inch cake pan. Bake at 350° for 30
minutes; cool, frost, and serve.

Carob-Currant Cake

Butter   ½ cup
Raw honey   1½ cups
Whole wheat pastry flour   2½ cups
Baking powder   1 teaspoon
Baking soda   ½ teaspoon
Sea salt   ¼ teaspoon
Carob powder   ½ cup
Eggs   2, beaten
Water   ⅔ cup
Vanilla   2 teaspoons
Cloves   a dash
Currants   ¾ cup
Walnuts   ½ cup chopped, plus decoration (optional)
Basic Spreadable Frosting (see Index)   (optional)

Cream butter; drizzle in honey and continue creaming until mixture is light and fluffy. Sift together the next 5 ingredients; gradually add to creamed mixture. Stir in eggs, water, and vanilla; mix well and fold in cloves, currants, and walnuts. Pour batter into an oiled and floured, square 8-inch pan and bake at 350° for 40 minutes. Cool and frost; decorate with additional walnuts.

Gingerbread

My neighbor always makes a double batch of this gingerbread since one never seems to last long enough.

Boiling water   ½ cup
Oil   ½ cup
Raw sugar   ½ cup
Blackstrap molasses   ½ cup
Egg   1
Whole wheat pastry flour   1½ cups
Sea salt   ¼ teaspoon
Baking powder   ½ teaspoon
Baking soda   ½ teaspoon
Ginger   ¾ teaspoon
Cinnamon   ¾ teaspoon
Whipped cream   for topping (optional)

Mix together boiling water, oil, sugar, and molasses. Add next 7 ingredients and stir well. Pour batter into a waxed paper-lined 8 by 8-inch baking pan and bake at 350° for 35 to 40 minutes. Cool, then cut.
Note: This cake holds up well in brown bag lunches.

Incredible Fruitcake

Mixed glazed fruits   1 pound, chopped or
  Mixed dried fruits*   1 pound, soaked and chopped
Pecans or walnuts   1 cup
Raisins or currants   1 cup
Cinnamon   1 teaspoon
Allspice   1 teaspoon
Nutmeg   1 teaspoon
Mace   ½ teaspoon
Orange juice   ½ cup
Blackstrap molasses   ¼ cup
Brandy or brandy flavoring   2 tablespoons
Raw honey   ½ cup
Oil   ½ cup
Eggs   4
Whole wheat pastry flour   1½ cups
Sea salt   ¼ teaspoon
Baking soda   ¼ teaspoon

In a large bowl, mix together the first 10 ingredients; set aside. Drizzle
the honey slowly into the oil while whipping vigorously, then add eggs
and beat until fluffy. Mix in the remaining ingredients and blend well.
Stir in fruit mixture and pour batter in 3 paper-lined, 8-inch loaf pans or
12 paper-lined, 4-inch gift-sized pans. Place in oven along with a pan of
water (to keep fruitcakes moist), and bake at 300° for 1¾ hours. Cool,
wrap in foil, and refrigerate.
* You can make your own, using any combination of dried apricots,
pears, apples, peaches, dates, figs, and pineapple.

Family Christmas Cookies

This recipe became our traditional family Christmas cookie years ago when my aunt's mother first had us try them. They have remained a favorite ever since. They are also ideal gift cookies.

Butter   1 cup
Raw sugar   2 cups
Eggs   2
Vanilla   1 teaspoon
Buttermilk   ½ cup
Whole wheat pastry flour   2 cups
Unbleached flour   1½ cups
Baking soda   1 teaspoon
Sea salt   1 teaspoon
Pecans   1½ cups chopped
Red candied cherries   1 cup quartered
Green candied cherries   1 cup quartered
Dates   2 cups chopped

Cream together the butter and sugar; stir in eggs, vanilla, and buttermilk. Add pastry flour, unbleached flour, baking soda, and salt, then fold in the nuts, cherries, and dates; mix well. Chill batter for 1 hour, then drop by teaspoonfuls onto oiled cookie sheets. Bake at 400° for 8 minutes. Cool completely on wire racks before stacking. Makes about 8 dozen cookies; if you have a big family or terminal munchies, a double or triple batch is advisable.
Note: Don't be upset about the candied cherries. Tradition is not to be tampered with!

Gail's Health Cookies

Butter   ½ cup
Peanut butter   ½ cup
Raw honey   ½ cup
Eggs   2
Vanilla   1 teaspoon
Whole wheat pastry flour   ¾ cup
Pecans   ½ cup chopped
Raisins   ½ cup
Sunflower seeds   ½ cup
Wheat germ   ¼ cup
Noninstant powdered milk   ½ cup
Sea salt   ½ teaspoon
Baking soda   ¼ teaspoon
Baking powder   ½ teaspoon
Rolled oats   1 cup
Dates   1 cup chopped
Milk   2 to 4 tablespoons

Cream together the butter, peanut butter, and honey. Add the next 13 ingredients, plus enough milk to make them stick together without making them wet. Mix well, then roll dough into 1-inch balls; place balls on an ungreased cookie sheet and flatten with a fork. Bake at 350° for 15 to 18 minutes. Cool before serving. Makes 3 dozen cookies.

Hill Country Hartshorn Cookies

My grandma gave me this recipe, made with a leavening found only in drug stores. Ask for it under its chemical names—baker's ammonia, ammonium carbonate, crystalline ammonia—or under its traditional name—hartshorn. It is very powerful and makes great cookies.

Whole wheat pastry flour   2¾ cups
Unbleached flour   3 cups
Raw sugar   1½ cups
Cinnamon   1 teaspoon
Lemon juice   of 1 lemon
Lemon peel   of 1 lemon, grated
Large eggs   3
Hartshorn   ⅛ teaspoon
Butter   1½ cups, softened

Place pastry flour and unbleached flour in a mound on the counter. Make a well in the flour and place the remaining ingredients in the well. Knead the ingredients until they are completely mixed together, then roll dough out and cut out cookies with your favorite cutters. Bake on an ungreased cookie sheet at 350° for 5 to 8 minutes, depending on the size, shape, and thickness of your cookies. Cool before serving. Makes about 14 dozen cookies.

Note: You may chill the dough overnight and use it the next day; this improves the texture. You may also roll the dough into logs and freeze it for later use.

Grandma's Raisin Cookies

Raisins or currants 1 cup
Boiling water 1 cup
Butter 1 cup
Blackstrap molasses 5 tablespoons
Eggs 2
Vanilla 1 teaspoon
Whole wheat pastry flour 2 cups
Rolled oats 1½ cups
Baking soda 1 teaspoon
Sea salt ¼ teaspoon
Cinnamon 1 teaspoon (optional)
Almonds ½ cup chopped

Place raisins in boiling water and simmer 15 minutes, then drain raisins, reserving 7 tablespoons of the liquid. Cream together the butter and molasses, add eggs and vanilla, and beat until light. Mix in the remaining ingredients, plus raisins and reserved liquid; stir well, then chill 30 minutes. Drop by teaspoonfuls onto an oiled cookie sheet and bake at 350° for 10 to 12 minutes. Cool before serving. Makes 3 dozen cookies.

Buckwheat-Honey Cookies

Butter   1 tablespoon
Raw honey   ¼ cup
Blackstrap molasses   1 teaspoon
Egg   1
Carob powder   2 tablespoons
Baking soda   ½ teaspoon
Sour cream   ½ cup
Vanilla   1 teaspoon
Buckwheat flour   1 cup

Cream together the butter, honey, and molasses. Add egg and carob powder, and beat until fluffy. Stir in the remaining ingredients and mix well. Drop by teaspoonfuls onto oiled cookie sheets and bake at 350° for 15 minutes. Cool before serving. Makes 2 dozen cookies.

Carob Chip Cookies

These are the most successful and delicious cookies in my house, year-round. A double or triple batch is usually enough—for awhile.

Butter   ½ cup
Raw honey   ½ cup
Egg   1
Vanilla   1 teaspoon
Whole wheat pastry flour   1½ cups
Baking powder   1 teaspoon
Sea salt   ¼ teaspoon
Wheat germ   2 tablespoons
Carob chips   1 cup
Nuts*   1 cup chopped

Cream together the butter and honey, slowly drizzling in the honey and whipping until fluffy. Mix in the next 6 ingredients, stir well, and fold in carob chips and nuts. Drop by teaspoonfuls onto an oiled cookie sheet and bake at 350° for 12 to 15 minutes. Serve immediately, or cool completely and store for up to 2 weeks or keep frozen for up to 4 months. Makes 5 dozen cookies.
* Walnuts, almonds, or cashews are great; sunflower seeds are good.

Wheat-Carob Cookies

Butter   1 cup
Raw honey   1 cup
Eggs   2
Rolled wheat   1 cup
Whole wheat pastry flour   2 cups
Baking powder   1 teaspoon
Baking soda   ¼ teaspoon
Sea salt   ¼ teaspoon
Cinnamon   ½ teaspoon
Cloves   ½ teaspoon
Powdered vanilla*   2 teaspoons
Carob powder   ½ cup
Nuts   1 cup chopped

Cream together butter and honey, slowly drizzling in honey and whipping until fluffy. Stir in eggs and rolled wheat. Sift together the next 8 ingredients, then add to wheat mixture Fold in nuts and drop batter by teaspoonfuls onto an oiled cookie sheet. Bake at 350° for 12 to 15 minutes, or until lightly browned on edges. To enhance carob flavor, cool slightly before serving. Makes 3 dozen cookies.

* If you use liquid vanilla, please add it when you stir in eggs and wheat.

Note: These little cookies are great with ice cream, especially mint or vanilla.

Pineapple-Oatmeal Drops

Butter   ½ cup
Raw honey   1 cup
Egg   1
Cinnamon   ¼ teaspoon
Nutmeg   ¼ teaspoon
Crushed pineapple   1 8½-ounce can, undrained
Whole wheat pastry flour   1½ cups
Sea salt   ½ teaspoon
Baking soda   ½ teaspoon
Rolled oats   1½ cups
Nuts*   ½ cup chopped

Cream butter, then drizzle in honey and beat until light and fluffy. Add the next 8 ingredients, beat well, and fold in nuts. Drop by teaspoonfuls onto an oiled cookie sheet and bake at 375° for 12 to 15 minutes. Cool completely before serving or storing. Makes 3 dozen cookies.
* Walnuts and cashews are great; almonds and pecans are good.

Famous Brownies

Butter   2 tablespoons
Raw honey   ½ cup
Vanilla   2 teaspoons
Egg   1
Carob powder   6 tablespoons
Whole wheat pastry flour   1 cup
Sea salt   ¼ teaspoon
Baking powder   1 teaspoon
Milk   ½ cup
Walnuts or cashews   1 cup chopped (optional) or
    Sunflower seeds or carob chips   1 cup (optional)
Cloves   a dash (optional)
Carob-Flavored Frosting or
    Homemade Honey Ice Cream (see Index)   (optional)

Cream together butter and honey. Add vanilla and egg, and beat until light. Sift together the carob powder and flour, then add to honey mixture together with the salt, baking powder, and milk. Mix well, then fold in nuts and cloves. Pour into a buttered 9 by 9-inch pan and bake at 350° for 35 minutes. Cool, then frost, or serve warm with ice cream.

Heather's Brownies

My daughter, Heather, is used to my requests for help with a new recipe. This one makes thick, fudgie brownies and will soothe even the pickiest carob skeptic.

Oil   ¾ cup
Carob powder   ¾ cup
Blackstrap molasses   2 tablespoons
Eggs   4
Noninstant powdered milk   ½ cup
Raw sugar   1½ cups
Wheat germ   ½ cup
Whole wheat pastry flour   1¾ cups
Sunflower seeds   1 cup
Sesame seeds   ½ cup
Sea salt   ½ teaspoon
Baking powder   1½ teaspoons
Vanilla   1 tablespoon
Cloves   ½ teaspoon
Nutmeg   ½ teaspoon

Combine oil, carob powder, molasses, and eggs in a blender; whip until thick like pudding. Pour mixture into a bowl containing the remaining ingredients and stir until smooth. Pour batter into an oiled and floured, square 8-inch pan and bake at 350° for 1 hour, or until middle tests done. Cool before cutting.

Gingerbread People

Kids of all ages love to make these.

Pellet yeast   1 teaspoon
Warm water   ⅔ cup
Ginger   ½ teaspoon
Raw honey or blackstrap molasses   4 teaspoons
Oil   4 teaspoons
Sea salt   a pinch
Whole wheat flour   3 cups
Raw honey   for brushing
Raisins   for decorating

Dissolve yeast in warm water, add ginger and honey, and let stand 15 minutes. Add oil, salt, and 2 cups flour; beat well for 5 minutes, then refrigerate overnight in an airtight container that will allow the dough to double in bulk. Next day, punch dough down, then let it stand at room temperature for 15 minutes. Flour counter with remaining cup of flour, turn dough out onto flour, and knead until smooth and no longer sticky. Roll out dough and cut into gingerbread people. Brush with honey, decorate with raisins, and place on an unoiled cookie sheet; cover and let rise in a warm place for 30 minutes, or until light. Bake at 350° for 15 to 20 minutes, depending on the thickness of the gingerbread. Makes about 6 to 8 gingerbread people.

Sopaipillas

Pellet yeast   1 teaspoon
Warm water   ¼ cup
Egg   1
Noninstant powdered milk   1½ cups
Oil   ⅓ cup
Raw honey   ⅓ cup
Sea salt   ½ teaspoon
Cornmeal   1 tablespoon
Whole wheat flour   5 cups
Coconut, peanut, or other oil*   1 quart, for deep frying
Hot butter and honey, jam, or other topping   (optional)

Dissolve yeast in warm water; set aside 10 minutes. Mix in the next 6 ingredients plus 3 cups of flour; stir well. Cover and let mixture stand for 1 hour. Mix well, then add the remaining 2 cups of flour and mix well again. Turn dough out onto a floured surface and knead 5 minutes, or until soft. Return dough to bowl and let rise, covered, in a warm place until doubled in bulk. Punch down, turn out onto a floured surface, and roll out to 1/8-inch thickness. Cut dough into triangles with 4- to 5-inch sides. Heat oil until a small piece of dough sinks to the bottom, then quickly returns to the surface. Fry sopaipillas until puffy and golden brown; they will turn themselves over. You may find that chopsticks are very handy for taking these treats out of the oil. Drain and serve with hot butter and honey. Makes about 5 dozen sopaipillas.
* Coconut and peanut oil have high burning points and are more digestible than most oils.
Note: After dough is punched down, it may be stored several days in the refrigerator before using.

Puffed Energy Bars

Raw honey   2 tablespoons
Peanut butter   3 tablespoons
Puffed corn, wheat, rice, or millet   2 cups
Dates   1 cup chopped
Sunflower or sesame seeds   ½ cup

In a large bowl, combine honey and peanut butter; beat until smooth. Add puffed corn, dates, and sunflower seeds; stir well. Press mixture into an oiled, square 8-inch pan, chill, and cut into bars for great munching.

My Granola Bars

These make good snacks and will also pass for breakfast on the run.

Raw honey   1 cup
Peanut butter   1 cup
Wheat germ   ½ cup
Granola (see Index)   4 cups, plus as needed
Sesame seeds   ½ cup

Line a 15 by 12 by ¾-inch cookie sheet with waxed paper; set aside. In a large saucepan, heat together the honey and peanut butter over medium heat until mixture is smooth and steaming. Add wheat germ and 4 cups of granola, then stir in sesame seeds. Remove from heat and add additional granola until you can no longer stir, then pour mixture onto prepared cookie sheet. Cover with another piece of waxed paper and roll out the granola bars with a rolling pin until they are flat, even, and firm. Refrigerate, then cut into squares.

Easy Danish Pastry

Many people think there is some kind of magic to making Danish pastries. There is, and it comes from you! Try this easy way to make it and you'll see what I mean.

Pellet yeast   1 teaspoon
Milk   1¼ cups, warm
Egg   1
Raw honey   3 tablespoons
Whole wheat flour   4 to 5 cups
Butter   3 ½-cup cubes, well chilled and in 5 lengthwise slices each
Sea salt   1 teaspoon
Filling

Dissolve the yeast in warm milk, then stir in the egg, honey, and 2 cups of flour. Stir well, then gradually add enough of the remaining flour to form a soft dough. Turn out onto a floured surface and knead until dough is smooth, but still soft and pliable. On another floured surface, roll out dough into a 12 by 24-inch rectangle. Visually divide the dough into thirds the short, fat way, and arrange 8 butter slices in a checker- board pattern over the middle ⅓ of the dough, 3 slices in the top row, 2 slices in the middle row, and 3 slices in the bottom row (see illustration

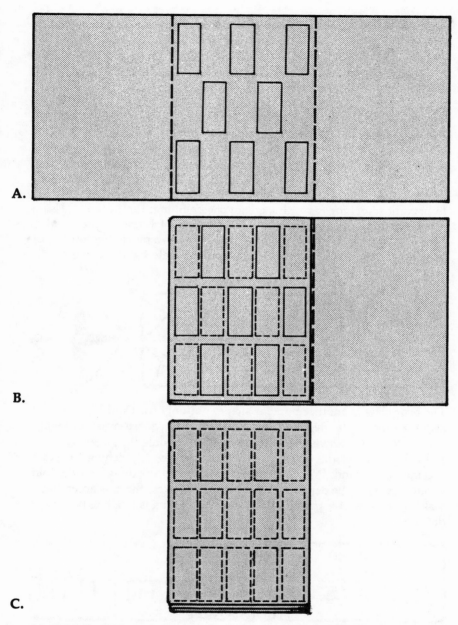

A).

B.

C.

A). Fold the left ⅓ of the dough over the middle, and fill dents with the remaining 7 slices of butter to form another checkerboard, 2 slices in the top row, 3 slices in the middle, and 2 slices in the bottom row (see illustration B). Fold the right ⅓ of the dough over all (see illustration C) and seal the edges by pinching dough together with your fingers. Roll out the dough again into a 12 by 24-inch rectangle; fold that in thirds and roll out again; repeat once more. (This gives you 45 layers of butter and dough!) Cut and fill as desired (see below), then bake immediately, without letting it rise, at 400° for 12 to 15 minutes, or until golden. Makes about 3 dozen pastries.

Danish pastries may be folded in a variety of ways; 4 of the most classic forms are also easy. In each case, about 1 tablespoon of filling is used for a 4-inch square piece of dough. Use more or less filling if you opt for a different size of dough.

The most traditional is the envelope shape, in which the filling is folded to prevent scorching (as with a cream cheese filling, for example). Using a 4-inch square of dough, place 1 tablespoon of filling in the middle. Now join the 4 corners of the dough together with a pinch over the top of the filling. When it bakes, the dough will separate lightly at the pinch, creating an attractive effect.

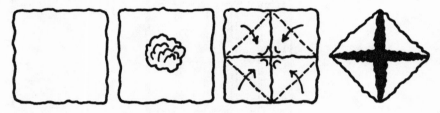

The bear claw is another popular shape, not only for Danish pastry but also for other rolls. Begin again with the 4-inch square piece of dough. Fill the dough lengthwise below the imaginary middle-line, keeping away from the edges of the dough. Fold the dough over, pinching the sides together all around. With a sharp knife, cut into the dough on the fold about 5 times at the depth of 1 inch. When it bakes, the cuts accentuate, making an attractive pastry, especially if the filling is made of berries or dates.

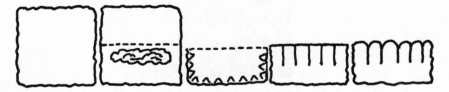

The "cozy" shape is very dainty. Using the 4-inch square piece of dough, place filling in the middle and pinch together 1 set of opposite corners. When this one bakes up, it looks like a cradle and also shows off the filling. Sliced, spiced apple or cherry filling is really good here.

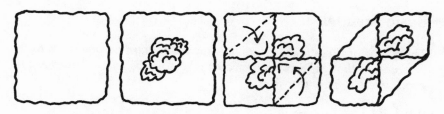

A light pastry with a hidden pocket of filling is another way to treat this dessert. Cut a 4-inch *round* of dough, fill the lower half-circle, and fold over the dough to make a half-circle. Pinch it closed, then bake as usual. For added interest, you may wish to lightly slash a design in the top. This will also keep the pastry from oozing filling from the seams.

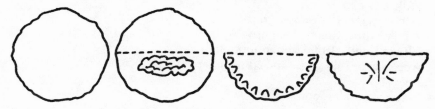

Fillings

Cream cheese—Whip cream cheese (or Neufchâtel for fewer calories) and use by the tablespoonful. A walnut and cream cheese combination also is delicious.

Almond—Almond paste can be purchased commercially. (The work involved in making it isn't worth doing it yourself.)

Applesauce Filling (see Index)

Chopped fruits—Bind these with honey.

Chopped nuts—Bind these with mincemeat.

Jam

Basic Strudel

This is one of those fancy treats that sounds so hard no one dares to try it. You can, though. Serve it to people who don't believe a dessert can be good unless it has sugar in it.

Pellet yeast   2 teaspoons
Warm water   ½ cup
Butter or oil   2 tablespoons
Raw honey   ¾ cup
Sea salt   ¼ teaspoon
Eggs   2
Milk   ¾ cup, warm
Lemon peel   1 teaspoon grated
Whole wheat flour   4½ cups
Gluten flour   1 tablespoon (optional)
Applesauce Filling (see Index) or other filling   3 cups
Egg   1
Water   1 tablespoon
Honey–Cream Cheese Frosting (see Index)   (optional)

Dissolve yeast in warm water and set aside 5 minutes, then mix in the next 6 ingredients. Add ½ the whole wheat flour and stir well for 5 minutes. Sprinkle in gluten flour if extra elasticity is wanted (especially if unbleached flour is substituted for whole wheat). Gradually add enough of the remaining whole wheat flour to form a soft dough. Turn out onto a floured surface and knead until smooth and elastic; remember, you will have to roll this dough out quite a bit, so you want it to be a little softer than if you were making bread—make sure there is enough flour so it isn't a sticky mess, but not so much that rolling out the dough becomes a full-time occupation. Let the dough rest several minutes, then roll out on a floured surface, getting it as thin as possible—⅛ inch is about right. If you allow the dough to rest between rolling times, the rolling will be much easier. Spread the filling over the dough, then roll strudel up like a jelly roll and place on an oiled cookie sheet. Whip egg and water together; brush on pastry to glaze. Cover strudel with a tea towel and let it rise in a warm place for about 45 minutes. Remove towel and bake at 350° for 30 minutes, or until golden. Cool, frost, and slice. Serves 8.
Variations: You may also fill the strudel with about 3 cups apple, cherry, or berry filling; cinnamon, butter, and honey filling; coconut, currant, and fig filling; or date, mincemeat, and sliced almond filling. For festive occasions, shape the strudel into a ring and decorate like a wreath.

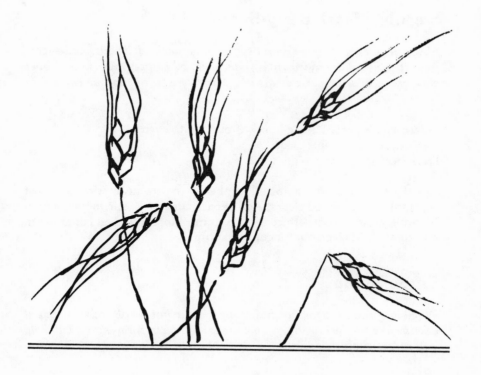

Toppings
and Other
Delights

Sugarless Fresh Berry Syrup

Many people enjoy this syrup because it is quick, delicious, and sugarfree. It is delectable on waffles, pancakes, or crepes, and is good over cheesecake or ice cream. It may be served fresh, or may be canned or frozen for later use.

Frozen concentrated apple juice   3 ounces, thawed
Tapioca flour   1 tablespoon
Fresh berries   2 cups

Mix together juice and tapioca flour; heat over low heat, stirring almost constantly, until liquid clears. Add berries, and cook, stirring moderately, until syrup becomes thick. Serve warm. Store in closed container in refrigerator. Makes about 3 cups of syrup.

Carob Syrup

Whether you use it for hot fudge sundaes or hot carob milk, drizzle it over a cake for decoration or over crepes for dessert, this syrup will help you forget about chocolate.

Carob powder   1 cup
Raw honey   1 cup
Sea salt   a dash
Vanilla   2 teaspoons
Water   1 cup
Cloves   a dash

Boil together the first 5 ingredients for 10 minutes over medium heat, stirring constantly with wire whip. Add cloves and simmer over low heat to 240° (the soft ball stage). Remove from heat and use immediately or store in covered glass jar in refrigerator. Makes about 3 cups of syrup.

Homemade Honey Ice Cream

Milk 1 quart
Heavy cream 1 quart
Raw honey 1¾ cups
Vanilla 1 tablespoon
Egg whites 6
Egg yolks 6
Fresh fruit, nuts, seeds, or other additions 2 cups

In a saucepan, combine milk, cream, and honey; heat to lukewarm, stirring constantly. Stir in vanilla, then chill. Beat egg whites until stiff, beat egg yolks until thick, then carefully blend whites and yolks together. Fold them into the chilled mixture, then pour it into your ice cream maker until ⅔ full. Crank away until the ice cream begins to set up, then add fruits or other additions. When the ice cream maker will not crank anymore, remove the dasher and place ice cream in the freezer for at least 1 hour to set up completely. Makes 1 gallon of terrific ice cream.

Basic Spreadable Frosting

This thick frosting is good for cupcakes, muffins, or layer cakes. Spread leftovers on graham crackers to make graham cracker sandwiches—my all-time favorite treat.

Butter ¼ cup
Cream cheese 2 tablespoons
Raw honey ¼ cup
Egg 1
Vanilla ½ teaspoon
Noninstant powdered milk about 1 cup

Cream together the butter and cream cheese, then slowly drizzle and beat in honey until mixture is fluffy. Mix in the egg and vanilla, then add enough powdered milk to make the frosting as thick as you prefer. Makes 1½ cups; enough for 1 layer of cake or 12 cupcakes.
Variations: For Spice-Flavored Frosting, add maple syrup or maple sugar, allspice, and nutmeg to taste before adding milk. For Lemon-Flavored Frosting, add 1 tablespoon of freshly grated lemon peel. For Carob-Flavored Frosting, add 2 tablespoons of carob powder, an additional ½ teaspoon of vanilla, and a dash of cloves.

My Honey–Cream Cheese Frosting

This is quite good on carrot cake, spice cake, or carob cake.

Raw honey   ¼ cup
Cream cheese   8 ounces
Egg white   1
Vanilla   ½ teaspoon

Cream honey and cream cheese together. Beat the egg white until it forms stiff peaks, then fold into creamed mixture. Add vanilla and mix until smooth. Makes 1 cup; enough for 1 layer of cake, 12 cupcakes, or 1 standard 8-inch loaf.

Honey Frosting

Raw honey   ½ cup
Raw sugar   ½ cup
Water   ¼ cup
Egg whites   2
Sea salt   a dash
Vanilla   1 teaspoon

Combine honey, sugar, and water in a saucepan, stirring only until sugar and honey are dissolved; heat over medium heat to 240° (the soft ball stage). Whip egg whites until stiff, add salt, then slowly drizzle in the hot syrup, whipping constantly until thick. Add vanilla and continue whipping until frosting reaches the consistency you prefer. Makes 1½ to 2 cups; enough for 1 layer of cake, 12 cupcakes, or 1 standard 8-inch loaf.

Applesauce Filling

Applesauce   ½ cup
Lemon juice   1 teaspoon
Whole wheat pastry flour   1 tablespoon
Honey   1 tablespoon
Cinnamon, nutmeg, cloves, or other spices   to taste
Nuts   to taste, chopped

Simmer first 5 ingredients together until mixture is slightly thickened Add nuts. Makes about ⅔ cup.

Honey Butter

Honey Butter is a terrific spread for toast, muffins, waffles, pancakes, and other goodies.

Raw honey ½ cup
Butter ½ cup

Cream the butter; add honey slowly and whip until fluffy. Store in a serving tub in the refrigerator. Makes about 1 cup.

Fresh Fruit Jam

Fruit juice ½ cup
Raw honey 1 cup
Agar flakes 1 tablespoon
Fresh fruit 2 cups peeled, sliced, and solidly packed
Lemon juice 1½ teaspoons

Boil together juice, honey, and agar flakes over medium heat, stirring occasionally (please do not use a metal spoon), until liquid is clear. Add the fruit and lemon juice, and simmer several minutes over low heat, stirring only occasionally. Pour jam into sterile jars and seal or freeze. Makes 3 pints of jam.
Note: If the jam is not as thick as you like it, you may adjust the recipe by adding more agar flakes while the jam is simmering.

Apricot-Pineapple-Cantaloupe Preserves

Fresh apricots 8 cups mashed
Fresh or canned pineapple 4 cups chopped and drained
Fresh cantaloupe 4 cups mashed
Raw honey 2 cups

In saucepan, mash apricots, pineapple, and cantaloupe together; add honey and simmer over low heat, stirring occasionally (please do not use a metal spoon) until mixture reaches thickness you prefer. Pour into sterile jars and store in freezer. Serve on hot biscuits, muffins, or bread. Makes 7 to 8 pints.

U.S. and Metric Measurements

Approximate conversion formulas are given below for commonly used U.S. and metric kitchen measurements.

Teaspoons	x	5	=milliliters
Tablespoons	x	15	=milliliters
Fluid ounces	x	30	=milliliters
Fluid ounces	x	0.03	=liters
Cups	x	240	=milliliters
Cups	x	0.24	=liters
Pints	x	0.47	=liters
Dry pints	x	0.55	=liters
Quarts	x	0.95	=liters
Dry quarts	x	1.1	=liters
Gallons	x	3.8	=liters
Ounces	x	28	=grams
Ounces	x	0.028	=kilograms
Pounds	x	454	=grams
Pounds	x	0.45	=kilograms
Milliliters	x	0.2	=teaspoons
Milliliters	x	0.07	=tablespoons
Milliliters	x	0.034	=fluid ounces
Milliliters	x	0.004	=cups
Liters	x	34	=fluid ounces
Liters	x	4.2	=cups
Liters	x	2.1	=pints
Liters	x	1.82	=dry pints
Liters	x	1.06	=quarts
Liters	x	0.91	=dry quarts
Liters	x	0.26	=gallons
Grams	x	0.035	=ounces
Grams	x	0.002	=pounds
Kilograms	x	35	=ounces
Kilograms	x	2.2	=pounds

Temperature Equivalents

Fahrenheit	−32	x5	÷9	=Celsius
Celsius	x9	÷5	+32	=Fahrenheit

Other Cookbooks from Pacific Search Press

The Apple Cookbook by Kyle D. Fulwiler
Asparagus: The Sparrowgrass Cookbook by Autumn Stanley
The Berry Cookbook by Kyle D. Fulwiler
Bone Appétit! Natural Foods for Pets by Frances Sheridan Goulart
The Carrot Cookbook by Ann Saling
The Crawfish Cookbook by Norma S. Upson
The Dogfish Cookbook by Russ Mohney
The Eggplant Cookbook by Norma S. Upson
The Green Tomato Cookbook by Paula Simmons
Mushrooms 'n Bean Sprouts: A First Step for Would-be Vegetarians
    by Norma M. MacRae, R.D.
My Secret Cookbook by Paula Simmons
The Natural Fast Food Cookbook by Gail L. Worstman
The Natural Fruit Cookbook by Gail L. Worstman
Rhubarb Renaissance: A Cookbook by Ann Saling
Roots & Tubers: A Vegetable Cookbook
    by Kyle D. Fulwiler
The Salmon Cookbook by Jerry Dennon
Starchild & Holahan's Seafood Cookbook
    by Adam Starchild and James Holahan
Warm & Tasty: The Wood Heat Stove Cookbook
    by Margaret Byrd Adams
Wild Mushroom Recipes by Puget Sound Mycological Society
The Zucchini Cookbook by Paula Simmons

Index

U.S. Equivalents

1 teaspoon	= ⅓ tablespoon
1 tablespoon	= 3 teaspoons
2 tablespoons	= 1 fluid ounce
4 tablespoons	= ¼ cup or 2 ounces
5⅓ tablespoons	= ⅓ cup or 2⅔ ounces
8 tablespoons	= ½ cup or 4 ounces
16 tablespoons	= 1 cup or 8 ounces
⅜ cup	= ¼ cup plus 2 tablespoons
⅝ cup	= ½ cup plus 2 tablespoons
⅞ cup	= ¾ cup plus 2 tablespoons
1 cup	= ½ pint or 8 fluid ounces
2 cups	= 1 pint or 16 fluid ounces
1 liquid quart	= 2 pints or 4 cups
1 liquid gallon	= 4 quarts

Metric Equivalents

1 milliliter	= 0.001 liter
1 liter	= 1000 milliliters
1 milligram	= 0.001 gram
1 gram	= 1000 milligrams
1 kilogram	= 1000 grams